Mark R

Pla

Mother Clap's Molly House, Product, The Cut, Citizenship, pool (no water)

Mother Clap's Molly House: 'Ravenhill's writing is tough, eloquent, sardonic, with some of the barbed formality of the Restoration style, which gets brutally peeled off in the present-day scenes . . . The message of this play is not "Come out," but "Come in." See if you can take it.' *Sunday Times*

Product 'is about selling and power: the power of the market place, the power of the images the Hollywood dream factory churns, the power to manipulate the individual and the masses, the power to romanticise things, even al-Qaida and eighty-per-cent burns.' *Guardian*

The Cut: 'This is a contemplative work that considers society from the oblique angle of a terrifying and hardly intelligible dystopia . . . *The Cut* is a fascinating, thought-provoking play that will leave its audience thinking deeply about what is said on stage and far more so about what is not.' *British Theatre Guide*

Citizenship: 'Ravenhill's hilarious *Citizenship* delights in the absurd whimsicality and fabricated self-assurance of preening, fumbling youth.' *Daily Mail*

pool (no water): 'A visceral and shocking new play about the fragility of friendship and the jealousy and resentment inspired by success.' *British Arts Council*

Mark Ravenhill was born in Haywards Heath, West Sussex, in 1966. Literary Manager of Paines Plough between December 1995 and June 1997, he was appointed Artistic Associate at the National Theatre in the summer of 2002. His first full-length play, *Shopping and Fucking*, produced by Out of Joint and the Royal Court Theatre, opened at the Royal Court Theatre Upstairs in September 1996. His other works include *Faust is Dead* (national tour, 1997); *Sleeping Around*, a joint venture with three other writers (Salisbury Playhouse, 1998); *Handbag* (Lyric Hammersmith Studio, 1998); *Some Explicit Polaroids* (Theatre Royal, Bury St Edmunds, 1999); *Mother Clap's Molly House* (National Theatre, 2001); *Totally Over You* (National Theatre, 2003); *Product* (Traverse Theatre, Edinburgh, 2005); *The Cut* (Donmar Warehouse, London, 2006); *Citizenship* (National Theatre, 2006); *pool (no water)* (Lyric Hammersmith, 2006); and *Shoot/Get Treasure/Repeat* (Edinburgh Festival, 2007, awarded both the Fringe First and Spirit of the Fringe Awards).

by the same author

Faust is Dead
Handbag
Shoot/Get Treasure/Repeat
Shopping and Fucking
Sleeping Around (*co-authored*)
Some Explicit Polaroids
Totally Over You

RAVENHILL PLAYS: I
(Shopping and Fucking, Faust is Dead,
Handbag, Some Explicit Polaroids)

MARK RAVENHILL

Plays: 2

Mother Clap's Molly House
Product
The Cut
Citizenship
pool (no water)

with an introduction by the author

Methuen Drama

METHUEN DRAMA CONTEMPORARY DRAMATISTS

1 3 5 7 9 10 8 6 4 2

This collection first published in Great Britain in 2008
by Methuen Drama

Methuen Drama
A & C Black Publishers Limited
38 Soho Square
London W1D 3HB

ISBN: 978 1 4081 0679 2

A CIP catalogue record for this book is available from the British Library

Typeset by Country Setting, Kingsdown, Kent
Printed and bound in Great Britain by
CPI Cox & Wyman, Reading, RG1 8EX

Contents

Mark Ravenhill
Chronology

September 1996   *Shopping and Fucking*, Out of Joint and the Royal Court Theatre (Royal Court Theatre Upstairs and national tour)

April 1997   *Faust is Dead*, Actors' Touring Company (Lyric Hammersmith Studio and national tour)

February 1998   *Sleeping Around*, a joint venture with three other writers (Salisbury Playhouse, transferred to the Donmar Warehouse and national tour)

September 1998   *Handbag*, Actors' Touring Company (Lyric Hammersmith Studio and national tour)

September 1999   *Some Explicit Polaroids*, Out of Joint (New Ambassadors Theatre and national tour)

May 2000   *North Greenwich*, Paines Plough (Wild Lunch series)

August 2001   *Mother Clap's Molly House* (Lyttelton, National Theatre, transferred to the Aldwych Theatre, February 2003)

July 2003   *Totally Over You*, performed as part of 'Shell Connections' Youth Theatre Festival (National Theatre)

March 2004   *Moscow* (Royal Court International Playwrights' Season)

October 2004   *Education*, read as part of 'National Headlines' season of topical verbatim monologues (National Theatre)

August 2005   *Product*, Paines Plough (Traverse Theatre, Edinburgh, and international tour)

Introduction

Over a century ago, Oscar Wilde reported with detached amusement – and his usual calculated provocation – on the working methods of the novelist Émile Zola. The great naturalist, Wilde observed with horror, spent months researching any new novel. If Zola was going to write about Parisian slums he went to live there! Wilde declared that he himself was an altogether different kind of an artist. Even a morning in the British Library reading about a subject would kill his interest and he could no longer write about it.

I'm a huge admirer of Émile Zola's work. Wilde offers a crude reduction of the French master's methods. Zola did indeed spend up to a year filling notebooks with statistics and observations before beginning work on each of his novels. But once work began, Zola drew heavily on his imagination and emotion to create fictions that resonate with dense, often sensual, imagery which goes far beyond any crude naturalism.

When it comes to my own work I do find myself more in Oscar's camp than Émile Zola's. I do very little research. This is probably a weakness in a contemporary British writing landscape where novelists and playwrights often compete to prove how thoroughly they've studied the real world before they sit down to write. But I have to say, rather like Wilde, that I finding knowing too much or pretty much anything at all about a subject before I write a play is a great hindrance.

The plays in this volume are almost entirely the result of my sitting at a desk. Here I wrestle word and action into some kind of shape. It's this shape which, when performed by good actors, allows me – and I hope you – to go out into the world and ask some new questions of it. So I hope you feel that you've got your money's worth from this volume even if very few interviews were conducted, reading lists compiled or site visits organised in the making of it.

Mother Clap's Molly House comes closest to a researched play. In 1998, at the Bodleian Library, I requested original documents about early eighteenth-century gay subculture. A wave of moral panic spread through London in the late 1720s, leading to raids on molly houses – meeting places for

gay men. So we now have a series of sensational reports of
the trials of mollies, a popular contemporary nickname for
homosexuals. I made a huge list of books I needed to study –
a year's worth of reading – and looked at the piece of paper
glumly for several months without inspiration. Finally
deciding this was never going to work – and after reading
one brief introduction to everyday life in London in 1700 –
I wrote the play. Subsequent drafts were enlivened by work
with students at LAMDA and their principal Peter James,
my ever-patient musical collaborator Matthew Scott, the
actor Bette Bourne, whose memories of living in a drag
commune in the 1970s seemed remarkably close to a modern
molly house experience, and Nicholas Hytner who directed
the National Theatre production of the play. I can't claim
any great historical accuracy for my play – for that I would
recommend you read Rictor Norton's definitive historical
study for Chalford Press; what I've written is a fantasia on
historical themes which I hope asks fresh questions about
sexuality and the market place.

The Cut is a work of pure imagination. For years it has
struck me that the Waterloo street of such bourgeois cultural
delights as the Old Vic Theatre has an extremely curt and
brutal name. Challenged by the theatre company Paines
Plough to write a short play inspired by a south London
street name, I wrote the first, considerably shorter, draft
of the play. Following illuminating discussions with Lucy
Morrison and John Tiffany at Paines Plough, the full-length
play stewed in my mind for over a year before I wrote it
down. I was inspired in part by the huge emotional and vocal
resources of Deborah Findlay, who had recently played
Mother Clap at the National Theatre, and I found writing
for a great actor pushed me into new territory as a writer.
A word of advice: try not to worry too hard about what 'the
cut' is as you read or see the play; it's a hidden fear and you
might find several things creep into your mind. See what
political, emotional or philosophical resonances the play has
for you. It's different for everyone.

Writing a play for and about young people is a challenging
experience and, once again, there is a pressure, if only from

oneself, to go out and interview young people, spend time with them and develop material through workshop and discussion. And yet by now I had enough of a sense of myself as a writer to know this was a sure way to kill a play stone dead. When Suzi Graham-Adriani asked me to write for the National Theatre's 'Connections' programme, I decided to write about teenage sexuality. The sexualised teenager is a recurrent icon in the global marketplace. Fears about children and sex are everywhere, and yet unsensational, clear-eyed writing is still pretty rare. But I had to face the fact I was nearer forty than fourteen. I dived into the world of the play based on a mixture of memories of school and conversations overheard on Camden buses at school clearing-out time. I was delighted and surprised when teenagers at the National Theatre's Young Company, and in subsequent school productions, declared it to be an accurate reflection of their experience. Maybe by the time you come to the play some of the teen slang in it will make it seem a historical piece; the pain of taking a first step into adult sexuality will surely last a little longer.

The virtual monologue *Product* came about because of two impulses. Let's get the baser impulse out of the way first. In 2004 I saw several friends – Tim Fountain, Tim Crouch and Russell Barr – all perform self-penned monologues, and I found myself jealous of their ability to write and perform. I determined to do the same myself. The other impulse was one shared by many writers: the need to find a voice for the changed emotional and intellectual landscape of a new era – that of the so called 'clash of civilisations', 'war on terror' and post-9/11 world. I knew I was unable to produce a piece that illuminated the facts in any fresh way; but I was interested in the way we were redefining ourselves as Westerners even as we created a new 'other', the Muslim. Hollywood movies aspire, often with ridiculous portentousness, to be our modern myths, so this seemed the perfect form to explore the way in which new icons and clichés were being generated. My director Lucy Morrison not only steadily guided an amateur actor but also pushed me through many drafts of the script.

Writing for a dancer's body is such a terrifyingly abstract thing to do that it can leave a playwright reeling. When I began working on *pool* (*no water*) with Scott Graham and Steven Hoggett of Frantic Assembly, I knew their form of physical theatre would push me into a new way of writing. But I quickly found myself very lost. A few images – proffered by Scott and Steve – from the American photographer Nan Golding were enough to anchor me and take me into an exploration of the destructive nature of friendship and the relationship between illness and art. Scott and Steve proved to be as scrupulous with words as they are in shaping moves, and so the final form of the text came about because of my collaboration with them.

When he writes about one of his celebrated Lacanian analyses of a film, says the great Slovenian philosopher Slavoj Žižek, he tries not to see the film first. It spoils the beauty of his writing and it is more illuminating to see the film after he has made the analysis. I understand a little of what Žižek means. I've tried to do the same in these plays. They're not an attempt to study the world, pin it down and hand it over in a parcel to you. They're rather a guess, an approximation of what might be happening out there, and an invitation to you to go out and interrogate the world and your place in it. If these plays – whatever their weaknesses – go some way towards doing that, then I shall be happy. Enjoy yourself.

Mark Ravenhill
February 2008

Mother Clap's Molly House

Mother Clap's Molly House was developed with the following students at LAMDA (London Academy of Music and Dramatic Arts): James Adams, Samuel Barnett, Jack Bennet, Kieran Brew, Nicholas Burns, Louise J. Cox, Gus Danowski, Daniella Dessa, Henry Douthwaite, Felicite de Jeu, Will Huggins, Lisa Jackson, Marie Lewis, Daniel Llewlyn-Williams, Anna Maxwell-Martin, Tom McKay, Jamie Michie, Gavin Molloy, Claire Redcliffe, Francesca Rogers, Gary Shelford, Stephanie Street, David Sturzaker, Rebecca Todd, Leatsa Tsimbris and Aaron Woodman.

Thanks to Peter James, Cat Horn and everyone at LAMDA

Mother Clap's Molly House was first performed at the Lyttelton Theatre, Royal National Theatre, on 24 August 2001. The cast was as follows:

Mrs Tull	Deborah Findlay
Stephen Tull	Iain Mitchell
Martin, *their apprentice*	Paul Ready
Princess Seraphina	Ian Redford

Whores

Amelia	Maggie McCarthy
Amy	Danielle Tilley
Mary Cranton	Debbie Chazen
Mary Bolton	Katy Secombe

Working Men

Kedger	Jay Simpson
Philips	William Osborne
Thomas Orme, *their apprentice*	Dominic Cooper
Gabriel Lawrence	Con O'Neill

Deities

God	Daniel Redmond
Eros	Paul J. Medford

Josh	Dominic Cooper
Will	William Osborne
Charlie	Jay Simpson
Tina	Danielle Tilley
Tom	Paul Ready
Edward	Iain Mitchell
Phil	Con O'Neill

Other parts played by: Deborah Asante, Martin Chamberlain, Pamela Hardman, Luke Jardine, Tom McKay, Iain Pearson, Philip Ralph, Ali Sichilongo

Director Nicholas Hytner
Set Designer Giles Cadle
Lighting Designer Rick Fisher
Music Director Paul Frankish
Sound Designers Neil Alexander, Colin Pink

A slash in the dialogue (/) indicates the cue for the next
actor to start speaking, creating overlapping dialogue

Act One

'Opening Act One'

Scene One

Chorus
> When at first Our Father mighty
> Made the Earth and Sea and Skies
> Then Our Father great and mighty
> Made Man and gave him Enterprise.

God
> Enterprise, shall make you human
> Getting, spending – spark divine
> This my gift to you poor human:
> Purse celestial, coin divine.

London is revealed – a city of business and enterprise.

All
> Enterprise, come light our darkness
> Business, shape our heart and hand!
> Then – oh rich Our Father mighty! –
> Lead us to the promised land.

London vanishes to reveal:

Tally shop. A large number of dresses. Workbench.

Mrs Tull *at the counter. Enter* **Martin**.

Martin   Sorry I took so long only I –

Tull   Martin. Where you been?

Martin   Get thread like Master said only I –

Tull   Get thread? Get thread? Dun't take hour and more to get thread.

Martin   Well, see, I was gonna go up –

Tull   Weren't just thread, ask me. Weren't just errand. You was wandering again, wun't you?

Martin   No. No.

Tull   Thought so. Wandering. How many times Master told you: Boy, dun't you wander or you'll feel my fist?

Martin   I know but I wun't –

Tull   If there's one thing he hates most in the world it's apprentice boy who wanders. Where you go, Martin?

Martin   I dunno. I get lost easy.

Tull   Cos we worry when you in't back, see? See you might think: man, look after meself. But we think: boy.

Martin   Yes, Mrs Tull.

Tull   There's Mother and Father to keep a boy straying from the path and we in't Mother and Father but still there's a worry when you're off.

Martin   Yes, Mrs Tull. Master awful angry?

Tull   No. Master's . . .

Martin   He had a fit?

Tull   No. Just . . . Master's took peculiar. And Master's resting hisself. So I'm out the front today.

Martin   What? You? You're gonna – ?

Tull   Thass right. I'm gonna drive the bargains. I'm gonna write them in the book. I'm gonna . . .

Martin   Yeah?

Tull   Oh, Martin. Figures is hard, in't they? You make anything of that?

Tull *shows* **Martin** *the ledger.*

Martin   No.

Tull In't numbers terrible things? Dance around when I look at them.

Martin He shoulda taught you.

Tull No. See I'm Wife. And ledger's − well, he's always done ledger. But now −

Martin So what you gonna do when customer arrives and there's writing in to do?

Tull I dun't know. Muddle through. Don't you worry about me. I'll find a way. Now you. Out the back. Great deal of mending to do today. Them two whores we hired to yesterday got into an awful fight on account of them both going after the same customer − him being the only customer a-loitering in Covent Garden − and ripped the dresses awful. So you put that thread to good use.

Martin Yes, Mrs Tull.

Martin *goes to exit.*

Tull Martin −

Martin Yes, Mrs Tull?

Tull Nothing. Just . . .

Martin You frightened?

Tull Frightened? No. Watched him often enough, in I? Show the sluts the dresses. Bargain with the sluts. Write the sluts' money in the book. Can't be so hard, can it?

Martin No. Can't be so hard.

Tull Wish me luck?

Martin Good luck.

Exit **Martin.**

Pause. The shop bell rings. Enter **Princess Seraphina** *− a large man in a dress.*

Princess Hello. Hello. Howdeedo.

Tull   . . .

Princess   Looking for your husband.

Tull   . . .

Princess   I'm looking for work.

Tull   . . .

Princess   See. I have a good hand.

He picks up a garment.

This one's been hurried. Poor thread in a poor light I should say. And if you're working with poor thread in a poor light you gotta have great skill otherwise – Now this (*his own dress*) is my own work. Now you look at the way the lace meets the body here. Perfect match. And you compare that work (*the dress from* **Tull**'s *shop*) to this. No comparison. Heaven and Earth. Shit and silver. Come run your hand over it. See.

He takes **Tull**'s *hand and runs it over his dress.*

What do you think of that?

Tull   What are you?

Princess   Princess Seraphina. Howdeedo.

Tull   You're a man.

Princess   Thass right.

Tull   In a dress.

Princess   Thass right.

Tull (*calls*)   Stephen. Stephen. It's a man. In a dress.

Enter **Stephen** *at great speed.*

Stephen   Told you: no work here.

Princess   But my rates are fair.

Stephen   I'll call the watch.

Princess   No rates fairer than mine. No work better than mine.

Stephen   Then let some sodomite take you on. Let 'em look to their own.

Princess   I'm not a sodomite.

Stephen   Or molly or mary or ingle. Whatever you are.

Princess   No, no. I'm a man as ever you are.

Stephen   Listen to it. Man. Rigged up like that.

Princess (*to* **Tull**)   See, when I'm dressed in trousers I get awful vicious. I think the whole world's against me and I strike out with my fists. But in a dress –

Stephen   I don't want – no.

Stephen *staggers.*

Tull   Oh, love.

Princess   Please, I gotta eat. Not asking for charity. I'm a good worker.

Stephen   Agh. Burning. Agh.

Tull (*to* **Princess**)   You're gonna kill him.

Stephen   Agh.

Tull (*to* **Stephen**)   Sit yourself down. Thass it.

Stephen   Aaaaagggh.

Tull   You got no right. Come in here trying to kill him. (*To* **Stephen**.) Thass it love. Hold on. I'm here. I'm here for you. (*To* **Princess**.) You be on your way.

Princess   I'm only asking –

Tull   And I'm saying: no. See – good Lord made two natures. Him. Thass man. And then – bit of his rib – woman. Thass me. There in't no room for third sex. You're against Nature. No wonder he got burning in the head.

Princess   That in't me. Oh no.

Tull   Oh yes.

Princess   Burning in the head? In't me. Burning in the head? Thass pox. On account of all the sluts he's fucked, that is.

Tull   No no no. I in't listening. Go go go. You mincing dog. You swivelling no-prick. Out. Out.

She pushes **Princess** *out of the shop.*

Tull   Oh, Stephen. In't it a wicked creature? Wicked creature saying evil words.

Stephen   You did well there, me love, see him off. You're gotta be strong once I'm carried off.

Tull   No. That in't gonna –

Stephen   Oh yes. Wun't be long before I'm dead as dead.

Tull   No, love.

Stephen   More fits 'an ever now. Burning in me head night and day.

Tull   No – good Lord in't gonna carry off man of industry, man of business. It's the makers, it's the savers, it's the spenders and traders who are most blessed. In't no love like the Lord's love of business. Thass what you said.

Stephen   Listen. He's taking me cos . . . He's taking me cos I'm bad.

Tull   No. Good man.

Stephen   See, he loves business, what he dun't love is . . . lustful thoughts.

Tull   You in't had lustful thoughts, Stephen.

Stephen   Oh yes, my love. Multitudes of 'em. Night and day.

Tull   Then thass me to blame. Thass woman tempting you.

Stephen   No, me love, in't you. And I've done lustful deeds.

Tull   No, no.

Stephen   Oh, how can you be so blind? You must have seen —

Tull   Seen nothing.

Stephen   You must have heard.

Tull   Heard nothing.

Stephen   In't you even wondered? When I in't . . . took you for twenty years.

Tull   Thass the way with marriage. First year is always nothing but lovemaking, after that — blue moon. Any Old Wife'll tell you that.

Stephen   See — there's God of industry, yes. And he smiles on London now. Gonna make us greatest city in the world. But then there's — oh, love, I got Eros whispering in me ear all the day long.

Tull   Then you gotta fight him.

Stephen   And I try. God says: Make money. But Eros says —

Tull   You wanna buss a little love? You wanna take me? That what you want? Come. I know it in't much of a body but I'm willing. I'm yours, love, you must do with me as you will.

Tull *pulls up her skirts.*

Stephen   There's been others.

Tull   No.

Stephen   There's been hundreds of others.

Tull   What's that? Can't hear you.

Stephen   All the day long. Ledger? Ledger's a lie. There's been monies out to buy whores, monies out for trinkets for my sluts, there's been drinking and gambling with doxies, there's – That's why we in't got new stock. Thass why you're always mending. That's why we got so few customers.

Tull (*sings unaccompanied during the above*)
   Our rates are fair
   So climb the stair
   To Tull's, to Tull's, to Tull's.

Stephen   Listen to me. I'm gonna be struck down! I'm gonna die! I'm gonna burn for ever! One more lustful thought and I'm gone!

Bell rings. Enter **Amelia** *and* **Amy**.

Amelia   Well, will you look at this. New stock! (**Amy**) Thank fuck the good Lord has smiled on me at last. I'd almost given up hope. All the old stock's fucked and the only customers we see is a Lord who wants a whipping once a week and a Critic of Plays who promises to pay another day. And how's a whorehouse to thrive on that? But now this – oh, won't they come from miles around to fuck this?

Tull   Stephen –

Stephen   That's it, love. See to the customers.

Amelia   Every day I've been waiting for those bloody coaches to arrive from the country – and out they step – lame girls, starved girls, girls with fingers missing, girls with hair on their chins and breath like a fart – and then: out she steps. Come to Mother I say and here we are. Now then – Shepherdess for this one.

Amy   I never cared for sheep. Family's been shepherds for years. But – used to hear them bells ringing round them bloody beasts' necks and I'd think: fuck you. Wun't have to live like this much longer. It's the bells of London for me.

Amelia   Thass right. Gonna make your fortune in London.

Amy   Fortune? Dun't know about that. Fair amount, I reckon. Got a clean body, willing manner.

Amelia   Do you have a shepherdess?

Tull   Don't know. Stephen –

Stephen   Measure her first.

Amy   Mother always made my clothes.

Amelia   Well, I'm Mother now.

Tull   You miss her?

Amy   Oh no. I never cared for her. Shepherd's wife. Thass a stupid thing to be, isn't it?

Tull   She'll miss you.

Amy   Oh no. Fourteen children. One less'd be a blessed relief I should say. Though I was always the fairest.

Tull   Is that so?

Amy   Oh yes. They'd all say – from preacher to pigman – 'by God, that's a fair child' and they'd try for a fumble but I thought: no. For I shall be a whore in London and make my money and ride through here in a carriage and gob on you.

Amelia   Maidenhead too? Oh Lord, in't He smiling down on me today. Got a Sir Somebody willing to pay twenty guineas to feel a hymen snap and see the blood come.

Amy   Twenty guineas? Fuck me. Twenty guineas. In't it a marvel what a body's worth?

Tull   Is this the manner of thing you had in mind?

Amelia   No. I want higher on the leg, a cap, a crook.

Tull   Might have something out the back. If you wanna – (*To* **Amelia**.) He had a turn, gotta rest himself.

Exit **Tull** *and* **Amelia**. *Pause.*

Amy Well, I better . . .

She starts to take off her dress.

You ever been to the country?

Stephen No.

Amy Country's alright for a child. But then I grew, see?

Stephen Yes?

Amy Do you think I'll make a good whore?

Stephen Don't know.

Amy Don't you think I'm fair?

Stephen Fair enough.

Amy In't that a wonder? Twenty guineas take a maidenhead. Shall we look at it?

Stephen At . . . ?

Amy Oh, fetch a mirror and let's look at my little marvel.

Stephen No.

Amy Oh, here.

She has found a little hand mirror. She puts it on the floor. She pulls her skirts up to her knees and stands over the mirror.

Now open up and . . . no. Can't see it yet. I shall need you to hold the mirror higher. Here.

Amy *holds the mirror out to* **Stephen**.

Stephen No. Can't.

Amy Oh please, sir. You gotta help me. It's a grand day when a girl finds her body in't just eating and shitting, in't it? Day when a girl discovers she's a commodity.

Stephen But there's lustful thoughts.

Amy   Oh no. Ain't no lust in a whore. Just business. Thass why God smiles on 'em.

Stephen   My lustful thoughts.

Amy   In't much lust in just looking, is there? I shan't let you touch. Come.

She hands **Stephen** *the mirror. She sits on the counter, pulls up her skirts, opens her legs.*

Now, sir, look into me.

Reluctantly, **Stephen** *does so.*

See hymen?

Stephen   I don't . . . reckon maybe . . . .

Amy   Now mirror up and let's marvel at Katie Cunt together.

Enter **Tull,** **Amelia** *and* **Martin. Amelia** *carries a shepherdess dress.*

Amelia   Now isn't this just the thing? Quick, miss. Don't delay.

Amelia *and* **Amy** *exit to put on the dress.* **Stephen** *sees* **Martin.**

Stephen   Oh, back at last, are you? Wanderer returns. Well, I hope you give him sharp words. You spoil him with soft tongue. Can't make him your infant.

Tull   Yes, Stephen.

Stephen   Oh, wife, I know you wanted an infant.

Tull   Oh yes. We both wanted that. Infants.

Stephen   Hundreds of 'em, eh?

Tull   Hundreds? Oh. That'd wear a body out.

Stephen   Dozens of 'em. Calling out night and day. Mum Mum Mum.

Tull   Dad Dad Dad

Stephen   And that never happened but –

Tull   Oh, I wanted to hold on to 'em. Wanted that more than all the world. Just my body never could.

Stephen   Don't fret yourself, love.

Tull   Heart said kid. Head said kid. Just Body could never hold on for more 'an a month.

Enter **Amelia** *and* **Amy** *in the shepherdess outfit.*

Amy   Oh, dun't I look wonderful? They'll all be standing to attention when I walks past.

Amelia   At last. Back in business.

Stephen *clutches at his head.*

Amy (*recites*)
    Lost sir lost sir searching high and low
    Looking for my sheep sir – oh where did they go?
    Oh pity me, oh pity me – a poor simple Jill
    Who only wants a flock sir
    To drive up her hill.

Stephen   Aaagh.

Amelia   I'll hire a boy. Run through the streets crying: Best fuck in London.

Stephen   Oh. Lust. Lust.

Tull   You gotta fight it, Stephen.

Amy   Oh yes. I'm the one they all want a fuck. Look at me. Look at my bubbies. Rise and fall. Rise and fall.

Stephen   Oh, love. Lord's gonna strike me down.

Tull   Think of ledgers, Stephen. Think of monies in. Monies out. Balance. Surplus.

Amy   There never was a girl like me. Oh, in't I wonderful?

Amelia   He'll cry: Come and fuck her each and everyone.

Tull   Figures. Numbers. Stock.

Amy   Cunt. Cunt. Cunt. In't I got a wonderful cunt?

Stephen   Aaaagggghhhh.

Tull   Don't let it into your head.

Amy   Look up me. Come into me. Work away. Make me whole.

Amelia   Good Lord, for what you have sent me – thank you, thank you.

Amy   Oh, the smell of me. Oh, the taste of me.

Tull *grabs the ledger – holds it up in front of* **Stephen**.

Tull   Numbers. Add 'em up. Total 'em. Carry 'em forward.

Stephen   Can't see 'em. Dancing.

Amy   How do you want me? Forwards? Backwards? Bring your friends, bring your family, cos Amy's here.

Stephen   Aaagggh.

Tull *flies at* **Amy**, *hitting her with the ledger*.

Tull   Stop that, miss. Just you – stop that.

Amelia   Mind my stock. Don't damage the goods.

Tull   Cover your mouth, girl. That's evil. That's muck.

Amy   Old woman. You're dry. I'm wet. In't that right, sir? I'm moist. (*To* **Martin**.) Come on, boy, you want me? Oh, there's me flock. Baaa! Baaa! Baaa! Come, ram – tup away. Baaaa!

Stephen   Aaaaghh. Lord's coming for me now.

Tull   No. Stephen. Stay. Stay.

Stephen   Can't hold out much longer. Aaaaagggh!

Tull   You gotta live, love.

Stephen   Aaagggh. Quick – you gotta listen. Running the business. So much to tell you. Quick. Aaaagh. Lessons to give you.

Stephen *collapses.*

Tull   Stephen – no.

Stephen   Ledger's yours now, love. Shop's yours. Aaaaggggh.

Tull   But, Stephen, I don't know how. Stephen, I can't.

Stephen   Aaaaggggh.

Stephen's *body convulses several times and is then still. Pause.*

Tull   Come on, love. You gotta come and teach me, love. Love. Can't go 'til I'm ready. Not ready to be alone. Love. Love. I'm here for you, love. Stephen. Stop that. You're a good man. Oh Lord.

Pause.

Amy   It weren't me, was it?

Scene Two

'Funeral, Motto 2 and Wake'

Chorus
   The Widow's in a sorry state
   With Husband dead and gone
   But tears won't bring back
   Milk that's spilt
   And *The Widow Carries On.*

The tally shop. A wake. **Stephen Tull**'s *body lies in an open coffin. A large number of people – men and women – among them the whores – including* **Amelia**, **Amy**, **Cranton** *and* **Bolton**. **Amy** *is still in the shepherdess outfit. They've all been drinking* *heavily for some time. A couple of musicians play. People are dancing drunkenly. Enter* **Martin**.

Martin   Ho there. Ho there.

Music stops.

Widow says: Thank you for coming. But now she's took to her bed.

Amelia   Oh no, that isn't right.

Martin   Took to her bed and she in't coming out.

Amelia   Widow's gotta join the wake.

Mourners agree.

Martin   Thass what she says and she says: Go home now.

Amelia   What? Quick jig and a mug of ale and off we go. Oh no. Dance 'til you drop. Drink 'til you reel. More beer –

Martin   No. You gotta go.

Bolton   Beer, boy, beer.

Martin   There in't no more.

Amelia   And strike up there.

The band starts 'Wake 2', but **Martin** *shouts them down.*

Martin   No!

The band stops.

Bolton   Bit of pleasure. Thass all we want.

Cranton   Shit old life. Wake comes along, you gotta make the most of it.

Bolton   You wanna enjoy yourself, boy. Tally shop in't gonna last long, you ask me.

Martin   Oh no. Carrying on. You'll see.

Cranton   You wanna look for a new trade, boy. Less you wanna starve. Who's got a head for business? Not her. Not you.

Amelia   Come on, boy. Dance while you can. Music!

The band plays 'Wake 3', the mourners dance. Finally, **Tull** *enters.*

Tull   Thass enough now. Time to go. Finished now.

Silence.

See, it's just me and him now. Thass proper way to send him off. Always said to me: 'My love, the rest of the world is either customers or thieves. And as long as we make sure the customers fill our purse and the thieves dun't snatch it, then what do we care for them? The world is you and me and there's an end to it.' So just you leave us be. I got a lot I want to ask him.

Amelia   D'you think he'll answer?

Tull   He'll find a way. Wun't you, love?

Amelia   D'you think you could ask him about new stock for the shop?

Tull   Oh no, in't that –

Amelia   See Sir Somebody is calling on our shepherdess tonight and once Sir Somebody has had her, then I'll have some capital. And I'll be looking to invest.

Tull   No. Tally shop –

Amelia   And I reckon dress up my old stock. Launch 'em afresh. Take these two girls. Rigged well –

Cranton   Oh yes, Mother. New markets for us.

Amelia   Rigged well they could fetch a fair price.

Bolton   Thass right.

Amy   That'll take work. Make these two fresh?

Cranton   Oh no. We was beautiful once. Wun't we, Mary?

Bolton   Thass right.

Amelia   So just you ask him where you can find –

Tull   No. That in't the manner of thing I had in mind.

Bolton   See, told you. Giving up the shop.

Martin   No. You in't gonna do that, are you?

Tull   I dunno. I wanna ask him –

Martin   But we gotta carry on, we gotta do that, there's new stock –

Tull   I gotta decide. Now leave us be. All of you. Just widow and husband and past and future to decide. Please.

They all start to exit.

Amelia (*to* **Amy**)   Come. Let's get you ready for Sir Somebody.

Amy (*to* **Cranton** *and* **Bolton**)   You must be in the next room and when I make a noise so – (*stamps on the floor*) – you must make a noise so: baaaa!

Bolton   Oh Lord. Who'd be a whore?

Exit **Amelia, Amy, Cranton, Bolton** *and the remaining mourners. Pause.*

Martin   You heard her. New stock and we'll –

Tull   Thass enough from you, boy. Leave a widow in peace.

Martin   Mrs Tull –

Tull   Peace.

Exit **Martin.** *Pause.*

Tull   Stephen. Speak to me.

Pause. Enter **Princess**. **Tull** *doesn't see him.*

Stephen, love. Wanna tell you, wanna ask you, Stephen.

Princess   Waste of time. Dead's dead ask me.

Tull   Oh no.

Princess   See when Mother died –

Tull   Dun't want to know about you! Dun't want to know about Mother!

Princess   Thass right. Anger. That's how it took me.

Tull   Is that right?

Princess   Vicious all me life I was. And then when Mother died – Lord, didn't know no bounds. Fighting. This un didn't look at me right, this un didn't speak to me right – smash 'em. Strike out with me fists. That how you feel?

Tull   Yes.

Princess   But then I think: Mother's dead. And I think: life goes on. And I think: put on one of her dresses.

Tull   That dun't seem right.

Princess   Thass what I thought. Dun't seem right. And I carried on: anger, fighting. But all the time dress is in a trunk calling me. And I thought: no, can't. Mother'll come back and tell me no.

Tull   Thass right. 'Thass my dress, son, and you got no right.'

Princess   But one day, feeling was too strong. And I went to the trunk and I put on that dress.

Tull   'No, son, no.'

Princess   And oh putting on that dress I felt such . . . peace and such calm.

Tull   'Don't you go swishing about, son. Gave birth to a man and a man's what I wants you to be.'

Princess   No. Never spoke to me. Cos she's dead and I'm alive and I worn her dress from that day to this.

Tull   We still got things to discuss. He'll tell me . . .

Princess   Now he's gone –

Tull   No.

Princess   I'd be good for the shop. See, I'm a character. Everyone loves a character. Everyone calls out to me: Howdeedo, Princess, and I call out: Howdeedo. And with a character –

Tull   Shop might close.

Princess   No, you gotta –

Tull   I need to ask him. Please.

Princess   Any time you want me, you just call out: Howdeedoo, and I'll come running.

Tull   I'll remember.

Exit **Princess**.

Stephen. Listen love. I been thinking and I . . . Oh, Stephen. I in't up to tallying. Little mouse, Stephen. In the dark with a needle, thass me. Little mind, little voice. Dry old, barren old body. I can't . . . Come back, love. Just a few minutes. 'Thass alright, my love. You sell the shop and move on.' Stephen. Please.

Enter **Martin**. *He carries a large bundle.*

Martin   Look! Look! Look!

Tull   What you got there, Martin?

Martin   New stock. Look.

He opens the bundle and pulls out some very grand dresses.

In't that wonderful? See? In't that something'll fetch a good price? And here. Now – you ever seen fairer than that?

Tull Where it all come from?

Martin Business'll take a turn with this, wun't it? Once word is out, we got this in stock, there'll be customers crowding in morning and night.

Tull Where you get it?

Martin It's what he would want. Business got to go on.

Tull They stolen goods?

Martin Dun't matter.

Tull Thought so. Martin. Thass wrong. Stolen goods.

Martin But that's business.

Tull Not this business.

Martin *sighs.*

Tull Or you'll swing, boy. That what you want?

Martin *shrugs.*

Tull Well, I'll make sure you do. Because I'll go to the constables myself, see?

Martin No you / bloody well won't.

Tull I shall. I love a hanging. I'll follow that cart through the streets and every rattle of the wheels I'll be calling: 'I told you so, I told you so.' Last thing you see as your neck goes crack will be me with a 'Didn't I say so?' on my lips. And there won't be no ballads or stories about you. Boy who stole dresses. Nobody'll remember that.

Martin You reckon? Then you do without me, see? You get by on / your own.

Tull Oh, I shall / I shall. I'll do that.

Martin You see how long you keep / going without me.

Tull You go back on the streets. You live like an animal. Go on. GO ON.

Pause.

Well, there's a fair old row, in't there?

Martin   You got a big old mouth on you.

Tull   Big as yours. Don't want to see you hang. Want you to take care of yourself, see? Because . . .

Martin   Because . . . ?

Pause.

You gonna write it in the book? Thass what Master always did.

Tull   I don't know how.

Martin   You'll work it out. Here.

Martin *gives* **Tull** *the ledger.*

Tull   Can't work it out.

Martin   Mrs Tull, you gotta . . . I'm looking to you. I in't Man, I'm Boy. Boy needs protecting, guiding, boy needs . . . Look after me. Thass your duty.

Tull   Love, I in't up to that. I'm frightened.

Martin   You wanna little beer, calm yourself?

Tull   Well, maybe I should.

Martin *goes to pour* **Tull** *a beer.*

Martin   None left. They must have been awful drinkers.

Tull   Right enough. More drinking than mourning I should say.

Martin   I could run and fetch you some beer.

Tull   Yes. A little more beer and then to bed. Here.

She gives **Martin** *a coin from her purse.*

Just mind you come straight back. You're an awful wanderer.

Martin   Don't mean to be.

Tull   I'd say to him: Oh, that boy's an awful wanderer. One day he'll wander off the edge of the world and they'll be no one there to catch him. Where do you go, Martin, when you're a-wandering?

Martin   Nowhere.

Tull   Take a lot of time going nowhere.

Martin   Nowhere special.

Tull   Well – jug of beer and then straight back. Thass straight back.

Martin   Voice big as that, you could run a tally shop.

Tull   You reckon?

Martin   Oh yeah. You can be Master now.

Tull (*laughs*)   Don't know about that.

Exit **Martin**. **Tull** *goes over to the stolen dresses. Picks one up.*

Well, in't that . . . Very fine. (*Another dress.*) Ooo, this'd fetch a good price. (*Another dress.*) Needs work but . . .

Looks at ledger.

Well and maybe I could . . .

Searches through ledger.

Goods in, goods in. Goods in!

Writes down first item.

Well and that in't a bad hand. Come on then, girl. Write 'em.

Scene Three

'Motto 3'

Chorus

    Apprentice boys go to the bad
    So watch 'em night and day
    And mark the scene that now unfolds:
    The 'Prentice Led Astray

Moorfields at night. Men silently cruise up and down. **Martin**
crosses with his jug of beer.

'Eros' song'

Eros

    Let Phoebus blaze it through the day
    His wagon burning bright
    For once diurnal course is run
    Comes Eros and the night.

    Arise you swain – no slumbering
    Oh heed the call of the night
    My arrow's sharp, my bow is stretched
    Here's Eros, here's delight.

    Arise! Arise!
    Up up and rise!
    And risen follow me
    And risen follow me
    And risen follow me.

    Let Eros guide you through the streets
    To ev'ry man a mate
    Oh fly my arrow from the bow
    Your passage true and straight.

    The prick of Eros' arrow's sweet
    It enters swiftly in
    And once sweet prick is known to man
    His pleasure can begin.

Oh come! Oh come!
Up up and come!
And coming think of me
And coming think of me
And coming think of me.

The tally shop. **Tull** *is working on the ledger by candlelight. Enter* **Martin**.

Martin   Know it was a long time. But Cook's was out of beer. So I went up James's and they was out of beer and –

Tull   All these years, Martin. All these years, working in this shop.

Martin   Then I went up Swinfield's and Stratten's but –

Tull   All these years and here was me never saw the beauty of figures.

Martin   I wun't wandering. Know it looks like – well, I weren't.

Tull   Come. See. Look at that. Just you look at that (*ledger*). Thass beauty, in't it? See that – down the page. Swelling, accumulating up . . . 'til . . . there. Total. Then carried forward . . .

Martin   What's that? That in't Master's hand.

Tull   Oh, you're sharp, boy. In't you the sharpest? Well, if it in't Master's hand must be . . . Come on. Come on. Work it.

Martin   Is it . . . ?

Tull   Thass my hand. Thass all my hand. Thass my ledger now. And this is my shop.

Martin   You decided?

Tull   I decided. We're carrying on, boy. On we go.

Martin   Oh yes! Yes!

He grabs **Tull** *and dances her around the shop. They both whoop. Then suddenly,* **Tull** *stops.*

You crying?

Tull   Crying? No. Just . . . tired. All them figures. Big responsibility I got now, innit? Bed for me.

Martin   What about the beer?

Tull   Take a cup up with me. Now – just mind you dun't go out a-wandering.

Martin   Oh no. In't gonna wander ever again. And thass a promise. Do a bit of work, I reckon.

Tull   Thass a good boy. You gonna miss Master?

Martin   Yes. . . . Thass a lie. No. In't gonna miss Master. You?

Tull   Course. Always.

Exit **Tull**. **Martin** *sits and sews. Enter* **Orme**.

Orme   This is a pretty place. It's all colours and shapes here, isn't it? I like that.

Martin   What do you want? You be on your way.

Orme   Which way?

Martin   Out the door.

Orme   But then what? That's the trouble with me. Don't know which way to turn. I turn this way, then I think: no that way. Turn that way, then I think: no, should turn the other way. Do you understand?

Martin   No.

Orme   That's a great shame. Felt sure you would. Saw you up Moorfields.

Martin   Oh yeah?

Orme   Just now. Walking up Moorfields. And down Moorfields. And up. And . . . Why's that then?

Martin   On an errand.

Orme   See you up Moorfields a few times.

Martin   Might have done.

Orme   You hear what they call Moorfields?

Martin   No.

Orme   Sodomites Walk. You never heard that?

Martin   Never.

Orme   Oh yeah, you take a piss up Moorfields. Take a piss against a wall and all of a sudden there's one man to the left of you and two to the right of you and they're all taking a piss too. And then one man'll reach out and play with the other one's prick. And t'other man'll reach out and touch your prick. Don't you think that's frightening?

Martin   What do you do?

Orme   What's that?

Martin   Man touching your prick. What do you do?

Tull (*off*)   Martin. Martin.

Orme   You ever have your prick touched?

Martin   No.

Orme   Well, you feel such shame and then you feel lost and you don't know which way to turn.

Orme *hides behind the workbench as* **Tull** *enters.*

Tull   Martin. Martin. Everything alright in here?

Martin   Oh yes.

Tull   Thought I heard – You muttering to yourself?

Martin   Might be.

Tull Well, don't. Enough tongues in the world without you sitting there wagging on the job. Shush while I sleep.

Exit **Tull** **Orme** *emerges.*

Orme That your mother?

Martin No.

Orme You act like she's your mother.

Martin No I don't.

Orme And she should like to be your mother.

Martin I've got work to do.

Orme Please talk to me. I'm still scared. Can't get it out of my head. Those men touching each other. And that man reaching out to me. Ugly with his lust.

Martin I don't want to know about that.

Orme Please.

Martin I don't want to know about you.

Orme Please. Don't say that.

Martin I want to get on with my work. Not right. Men wandering in the dark. Thass all wrong.

Orme Lost souls, in't they?

Martin Yeah. Burning up in Hell on Earth.

Orme But what they to do? No home. Mother and Father wun't have 'em. So – out into the night and . . . grope away. Give 'em a home and that'd all be different. Let your molly be a family. Let your molly be Father or Mother.

Martin Oh no. That in't possible.

Orme And let 'em live in a molly house. Thass what I say.

Martin That in't gonna happen.

Orme Oh no?

Enter **Kedger**. *As he does,* **Orme** *hides.*

Kedger You seen a lad?

Martin What sort of lad?

Kedger Small lad. Fair face.

Martin What is it? Thief?

Kedger Oh no. Not a thief.

Martin Murderer?

Kedger No. Apprentice. I upholster and he's my lad.

Martin Run off, has he?

Kedger No. Not run off. But he wanders. And then he gets lost. And then he gets into awful trouble.

Martin What sort of trouble?

Kedger You seen him?

Enter **Philips**.

Philips The boy in here?

Tull (*off*) Martin. I told you. No wagging.

Enter **Tull**.

Tull Oh. Shop's closed. Come back tomorrow.

Martin They're looking for a lad.

Tull Well, wrong place for that.

Martin Apprentice boy who's lost.

Tull Where you see him last?

Kedger Moorfields.

Tull Long way from Moorfields here. Why you come searching in my shop?

Philips   Saw him come down this way.

Tull   Well, only lad here's mine. In't that right, Martin?

Martin   That's right.

Tull   So you best be on your way. Can't distract the lad when there's work to be –

Tull *has been moving to the bench and now she discovers* **Orme**.

You. Out of there.

Orme *emerges*.

Tull   This the one?

Kedger   Thomas!

Orme   You gonna beat me?

Philips   No.

Orme   Oh please. I've earned it.

Philips   We've been worried to distraction.

Orme (*to* **Philips**)   Oh, Mother, forgive me.

Tull (*laughs*)   What's that you say, boy? (*To* **Philips**.) Called you Mother.

Kedger   This one of your games, boy?

Tull   You in't no mother.

Philips   No. But wun't do no harm if he wants to call me mum, will it?

Orme   Oh yes. Mother. (**Philips**) And Father. (**Kedger**) Because my real father was a beater of children and animals. And my mother was transported long ago for her wickedness. So now we must play at families. I'll be child.

Kedger   And I'll be Father.

Philips   And I'm . . . I'll play at Mother, for the boy's sake.

Tull   Don't think the Lord intended . . .

Orme   Lord intended each of us to have a father and a mother and if Nature don't provide 'em, we must do what we can.

Tull   Well, it dun't sound right to me.

Philips   Come. Back to bed.

Orme   Can we go up Bartholomew Fair tomorrow?

Philips   He wants to see the Rabbit Woman.

Kedger   With the rabbits coming out of her cunt? That's all a trick if you ask me.

Philips   Hush. Let the boy have his illusions. Grow up and he'll lose them soon enough.

Kedger   Alright then, Bartholomew Fair it is.

Orme   Oh, thank you. Thank you. (*To* **Martin**.) Will you come with us?

Tull   Oh no. He can't. Work tomorrow.

Orme   Room for one more, isn't there?

Tull   No time for pleasure. His head's filled with trade. In't that right, Martin?

Kedger   Then we'll bid you good night.

Tull   Good night.

Exit **Kedger**, **Orme** *and* **Philips**. **Martin** *goes back to his sewing.*

Tull   That's it. Work to be done. Man was put on this Earth to work. And if he don't he becomes awful effeminate.

Martin   Is that right?

Tull   Oh yes. Man who don't labour, man who don't produce, man who lies back and watches the world goes by, man like that gets awful womanish. Then no woman wants him and every man despises him and he sees out his days alone and despised. So just you mind that.

Martin (*mutters*)   Yes, Mother.

Tull   What's that?

Martin   Said: Yes, Mother.

Tull   Well, good. Me and you and Business now, boy, and thass all the world to us. So here's what we're gonna do. Work night and day. Dress up the old stock, in with the new. And then in with the customers. And you're gonna fit 'em and I'm gonna drive the bargains – and ooo I'm gonna drive 'em hard.

Scene Four

'Motto 4: New Stock'

Chorus
    New stock brings Tull new customers
    A penny earned brings more
    But still there's danger up ahead
    A Bargain With A Whore.

The tally shop. **Tull** *is helping* **Bolton** *into a dress.* **Amelia** *is watching.*

Tull   Thass it. Very fine.

Amelia   What a pleasure this is, my dear. See you back in business.

Tull   New stock's always a pleasure, innit? No pleasure finer I should say.

Amelia   The months passed and they all said: Tull's is closed and the widow wun't open again. But I said: No, just working up the stock. And here you are: open for business once more . Of course there's some as say you haven't got the head for it.

Tull   Oh are there now?

Amelia   But I tell 'em – no. Mind that one. Looks like a little pinched thing couldn't make boo. But that's deception. Punch yer teeth out to protect her shop, I say.

Tull   Well, in't you got the measure of it?

Enter **Cranton**, *in a dress.*

Cranton (*to* **Bolton**)   How do I look?

Bolton   Well enough.

Cranton   Feels good. It's a good cloth. Come. Run your hand over it. Here.

She takes **Bolton**'s *hand and runs it down the dress.*

See. Feels good, dunnit? Clean and fresh. And now I feel clean and fresh.

Bolton   Soon be spoiled. There's always mud and men to spoil a dress.

Cranton   But for now . . .

Bolton   You're a dreamer, girl. Dreaming's foolish in a whore.

Amelia   So. Come, Mrs Tull. Name your price. How much a dress a day?

Tull   Sixpence.

Amelia   Sixpence? Thass more than before.

Tull   Better stock than before.

Amelia   But sixpence . . .

Tull   What? Do you ask me for charity?

Amelia   No. Not charity. But favourable terms.

Tull   What terms?

Amelia   Threepence a dress a day.

Tull   Threepence? Threepence? Oh no. I in't doing that.

Amelia   Then we must look elsewhere. Come, girls, dresses off. Up Crawl's.

Tull   Well, maybe you better do that.

*Enter **Amy**, from rear of shop. She is struggling to get into a dress – an elaborate affair with a nautical theme. **Martin** follows her. **Amy** looks at herself in the mirror.*

Amy   Oh, but in't I fine? Knew London would suit me. Oooo – I'm riding the waves. Carrying my goods into port.

   Tossed sir, tossed sir, tossed by the sea
   Looking for a harbour – O lend a hand to me.

Tull   Oh yes. That's very fine. See, in't that good? Threepence a day? Oh no. You wanna pay a good price for that. Thass worth an investment. Martin – lace her up.

Amy   Stick me on front of a ship, I reckon. Sailors in the rigging, eyes on me. Wun't that be fine?

Tull   Thass the idea. Wants this dress, dun't you?

Amy   Oh yes.

Martin *is pulling at the laces on **Amy**'s dress.*

Martin   In't gonna go.

Amy   Pull harder.

Cranton   Oh, Amy. Is your belly grown? Mary, Amy's belly's grown.

Amelia   What's that?

Amy   Must be London.

Bolton   Must be men.

Amy   What you mean?

Bolton   When's the last time you bled, girl?

Amy   I don't . . . weeks . . . months maybe.

Cranton   And you in't wondered?

Amy   Thought . . . London. Good life. Thought maybe now I was earning Lord's saying: See, girl, you in't cursed no more.

Amelia   Well, that's spoiled goods now, innit? Fresh in with a bloom, I thought, but no – belly on her already. Thass your price halved, girl. Stupid, stupid child.

Tull   That's a blessing, baby.

Amelia   No. That's a curse.

Tull   Don't know what you're talking about.

Amelia   Baby? That'll suck the youth and the beauty and the life out of her, baby will.

Amy   Please. Don't want to be Mother.

Tull   You think that now.

Amy   No. No. Don't want it inside me.

Tull   You see. Mother's instincts'll come and then –

Amy   Mother's instincts? Don't want Mother's instincts. I in't a fucking animal.

Bolton   Baaaaa.

Amy   Bitch. Bitch.

Amy *lashes out at* **Bolton** *but* **Amelia** *holds her back.*

Amelia   Thass enough. I'm Mother here.

Bolton   Baaaa.

Amelia   And I say enough.

Cranton   Mother could sort you, couldn't you, Mother?

Amy   How you mean?

Cranton   Mother's got the art, in't you, Mother? See, when Mary's belly blew up –

Tull   No.

Cranton   Mother, will you fix her?

Amelia   If she pays the price I might.

Bolton   Pain's awful bad.

Amy   How much?

Tull   No. Don't you let them thoughts into your head. That's killing and killing's sin and sin's damned and damned's torment for ever. That what you want? No, you don't.

Amy   But I in't ready.

Tull   See, baby comes then Nature speaks to you.

Amy   No. Can't hear nothing.

Tull   Then listen harder. Cos there's women as spend their whole lives praying and praying for infants to come. Praying right to the day when their body dries up and Nature passes 'em by and there in't no hope left. So just you mind that. (*To* **Amelia**.) Dun't kill the infant.

Amelia   But business tells me kill it.

Tull   And I say don't.

Amelia   Can't afford to. Unless . . .

Tull   Yes?

Amelia   You could hire the dresses cheap. Keep down our costs. Then I could –

Tull   No. I can't.

Amelia   Then she can't hold on to the child.

Tull   Maybe I can . . . fourpence.

Amelia   Cheap? That in't cheap.

Tull   Three.

Amelia   No. Penny a dress a day.

Tull   Penny? I can't . . . penny.

Amelia   Penny or else we can't afford . . .

Tull   Penny and she'll keep the child?

Amelia   May God smite me hard if she don't.

Tull   Alright . . . a penny a dress a day.

Amy   But I don't want an infant.

Amelia   Good for business, girl, you're having it.

Amy   Oh no. No.

Amelia   Say thank you, girls.

Cranton/Bolton   Thank you, Mrs Tull.

Exit **Amelia**, **Amy**, **Cranton** *and* **Bolton**.

Tull   Well, better write in the book. Ledger, Martin.

Martin *fetches the ledger.* **Tull** *writes.*

Tull   Not the Big I Am now, am I? Oh, Martin. Numbers dancing again. What we gonna do? I can't bargain with a whore. Whores is hard.

Martin   New customers.

Tull   But who?

Martin   New stock there's gotta be . . .

Tull   Who but a whore's gonna hire to dress up as shepherdess or nymph in glory or Queen of Spain?

Martin   Gotta be someone.

Tull   Then we better find 'em, boy. And quick. Before we starve.

Scene Five

'Motto 5: Dame Fortune'

Chorus
> Dame Fortune spins her wheel around
> And lives are lost or made
> Just when she thinks that all is lost
> *The Widow Finds New Trade.*

The tally shop. **Orme** *at the counter. Enter* **Martin**.

Orme   Good day to you.

Martin   What you doing here?

Orme   Shop's awful quiet. Thought: he's bound to be working. Great bundles of thread and cloth. But you're idle, in't you? So come play, Master Idle.

Martin   I in't playing. There's no games here.

Orme   Come. Say I'm an old whore with a face of patches and a cunt of death. And you gotta rig me up cos the King's sent for me so he can take his pleasure.

Martin   She don't want you here. She says you're womanish. Says you're a snare. So you go back where you belong. Back into the dark. Up Moorfields. And wandering and groping and –

Orme   No. Cos – to speak true – Moorfields means nothing to me now. And thass your doing.

Martin   How so?

Orme   Now all I think about is you. And I try to get you out of me head. And I'm up Moorfields and it's: Whoever the fuck wants to fuck me, fuck me. And it's: The stranger the stranger I'm fucking the better. But then in the act and I close my eyes and still I see your face.

Martin   Yeah?

Orme   Yeah. So I had to come to you and tell you and win you. What do you say? Speak true to me. What's in your heart?

Martin   I don't know.

Orme   Heart's speaking. Listen to it. Listen. What's it saying?

Tull (*off*)   Martin.

Martin   Out. Out.

Orme   Oh no, I in't going out. But – round the back. Thass something I could do. You deal with her and I shall be waiting for you. Round the back way.

Orme *hides. Enter* **Tull**.

Tull   That customer?

Martin   No.

Tull   Well, you call if customer comes.

She turns to go. Bell rings. Enter **Amelia**, **Bolton** *and* **Cranton**.

Oh Lord. Whores in't welcome here no more.

Amelia   Dresses returned.

Martin   Three out. Two back. Thass wrong.

Amelia   Thass new girl. She's run off.

Tull   What's that?

Amelia   New girl. We in't seen her. She's run off.

Tull   In my dress?

Amelia   Well, it seems that – yes. Run off in the dress.

Tull   Then I'm gonna find her, see? I'm gonna find her and I'll get my dress.

Amelia   But what about these girls?

Tull   Fuck 'em. Bitches. Martin – you mind the shop.

Tull *starts to exit, followed by* **Amelia, Cranton** *and* **Bolton.**

Amelia   Can't let one girl's / selfishness spoil it for the rest.

Tull   You hire from the / tallywoman you return when due.

Bolton   But, Mother –/ what about us?

Cranton   Something popish for me, Mother.

Exit **Tull, Amelia, Cranton** *and* **Bolton.**

Martin   Thomas. Thomas.

Martin *searches for* **Orme. Orme** *emerges in a dress.* **Martin** *doesn't see him at first but then:*

Martin   Take that off.

Orme   There's a butcher. Comes a-wooing me tonight.

Martin   You best put that back.

Orme   Butcher comes. 'Oh, wash your hands. For aren't they covered in blood and won't they spoil my dress?'

Martin   Give it me.

Orme   And butcher says: 'I can scrub all I like but still there's blood on me. For haven't I spent a life in slaughtering of cows and pigs and chicks? There ain't nothing can ever wash away all that blood.'

Martin   Thomas.

Orme   'Oh, but red on your palms and red under your nails, it turns Kitty's stomach so.' 'Well, that's how it is with me and you must take me how I am.'

Martin   Off!

Martin *grabs* **Orme** *and tries to get the dress off him.*

Orme   Take care, Butcher, take care. For although I'm only a poor, sweet girl, I can put up a fight.

They fall to the floor.

Oh, Butcher, mind my lace. Mind my hair. Mind my face.

Martin   Not so strong now, eh, miss?

They lie still for a moment. They get the giggles.

Do you paint?

Orme   No.

Martin   But your skin is so fair.

Orme   As ever Nature made it.

Martin   And your brows are so fine.

Orme   As ever Nature gave me.

Martin   And your lips are the reddest as ever I saw.

Orme   Nature too.

Martin   No. No. I'm sure you paint.

Orme   I tell you I don't. Come. Taste 'em and see.

Martin *kisses* **Orme**.

Martin   You're right. No taste of paint at all.

Orme   Now – your turn. Now you shall be Kitty and I shall be Butcher.

Orme *starts to take off the dress.*

Martin   But – I wanna be Butcher.

Orme   But you can't be Butcher all the time. Sometimes you must be Kitty.

Martin   Why?

Orme   Because I want you to.

He holds out the dress. **Martin** *hesitates.*

You in't scared?

Martin   No. Just . . .

Orme   Then come.

He helps **Martin** *into the dress.*

The butcher's been waiting all day long. Smiling at the customers. And chopping at a leg and at a breast and stringing up a ham, do you know what the butcher's been a-thinking of? Do you?

Martin   No.

Orme   The butcher's been waiting for night to fall when his Kitty comes to him and work is over and pleasure begins. There.

Martin *is now in the dress.*

Orme   How do you feel?

Martin   . . . Foolish.

Orme   Don't look foolish.

He leads **Martin** *to a mirror.*

Orme   See. As pretty a miss as ever walked the world.

He kisses **Martin**'s *neck.*

Orme   Now – you ready for the butcher?

Martin   No. I want . . . I want a different game.

Orme   Yes?

Martin   Sisters together. You be Kitty and I shall be . . .

Orme   Hannah.

Martin   Hannah? Ugh. Never cared for Hannah. Susan. You be Kitty and I'll be Susan.

Laughing, **Orme** *starts to put on another dress.*

Martin   Now Susan – Susan is a lazy slut. For isn't her father a merchant and aren't all the riches of the Indies hers and doesn't she spend all her days lying back with a: Will it be the pineapple or the pomegranate today? With what shall I fill myself? Susan can't be stirred 'til one day there's a knock at her door.

Orme *knocks.*

Martin   And it's Kitty Fisher.

Orme   Her neighbour.

Martin   Her maid.

Orme   Neighbour.

Martin   Maid. Kitty, now I look at you, you're a very pretty thing.

Orme   Thank you, miss.

Martin   Do you like pomegranate, Kitty?

Orme   Ain't never had none, miss.

Martin   Then come taste, Kitty, come taste.

Martin *and* **Orme** *kiss. Enter* **Kedger** *and* **Philips**.

Kedger   Well, here's a to-do. Come looking for a lad and find two little misses. World of surprises, in't it, Mother?

Philips   More wonders in the world than we dreamed of, Father.

Kedger   Come, boy, home.

Orme   Two big brutes in our chamber. Oh, Miss, what are we to do?

Kedger   Thass enough, boy. Dress off and off home.

Philips   Oh, Father. Let him have his sport. For now I look at 'em they're very pretty girls.

Orme   Oh beware, sister, beware. For when men praise, in't they after your maidenhead?

Martin   Thomas.

Kedger   There's upholstering a-waiting, Mother.

Orme   Oh, sister, let us live out our days as virgins and as we go through Heaven's gates we'll lift up our skirts and say: See, our maidenheads are here. And they'll have kept a special place for us with all the virgins.

Martin   Don't wanna play this. He made me.

Kedger   Thass the way with the lad. Always a game too far. Come. Home.

Orme   I in't doing it. I in't.

Philips   Come now, Father's anger is up, Thomas.

Orme   No Thomas here. Just Kitty and Susan here. Kitty and Susan in love and no need for Mother nor Father. Oh, Susan, Susan.

Martin   No. Don't want you.

Orme   Don't hurt me, Susan.

Martin   Game's over now. Susan's dead and gone and Martin's back. So just you be on your way. Just playing, see?

Orme   Oh yes?

He grabs **Martin** *and pulls him up to the mirror.*

Tell everything in a face. Just you take a look. That's a molly face. And that body. You listen to it. Those hips screaming: molly, molly, molly.

Martin   Off me. Off me. Off.

Martin *pushes* **Orme** *away. Pause.*

Philips (*to* **Orme**)   Come, chuck. Can't force a body when the body in't willing.

He takes **Orme** *in his arms and kisses him.*

Kiss from Mother.

Kedger   An' a kiss from Father.

Kedger *kisses* **Orme**.

Philips   That better now?

Orme   Thought he wanted me.

Philips   I know, love. But now you've learned. Thass the world and if you wander in it it'll drown you in its lies and trickery.

Martin   Thomas – didn't wanna – I just . . .

Kedger   Come. Thass it. Kiss the lad and make amends.

Martin *kisses* **Orme**.

Orme   And now we're family, in't we? Kitty Fisher. Susan Guzzle.

Martin (*laughs*)   Guzzle?

Orme   Guzzle.

Kedger   It's ever a new game with him.

Orme   And Mother's . . . Miss Selina.

Philips   Thass a good un.

Orme   And Father's . . . Hardware Nan.

Kedger   Oh Lord. In't you the strangest child?

Orme   Kitty Fisher. Susan Guzzle. Miss Selina. Hardware Nan.

He runs around, throwing dresses in the air.

Come dress and play, dress and play. / Miss Selina – for you. Hardware Nan. What you gonna wear? Oh, dress and play. Dress and play.

Martin   Thomas. Take care there. / Thomas. Mind the stock. Thass – Thomas!

Kedger   Thass enough now, boy. / Thass too much.

Philips   Father – let him have his fun.

Orme *gives a dress to* **Kedger** *and a dress to* **Philips**.

Orme Thass for you. / Thass for you. Come dress and play. Let's all play families. And we're living in the molly house.

Martin No. Can't use the stock like that. Thomas.

Tull (*off*) You hire from the tallywoman, you return when you're due, see?

Martin Oh Lord. Can't be found. Out the back.

Orme Stand and face her.

Martin No. Out the back. Please. Please.

Martin, **Orme**, **Kedger** *and* **Philips** *hide behind the screen as* **Tull** *enters with* **Amy**. *They are pursued by the* **Princess**.

Tull See, miss. I won't be messed with. You return when due.

Princess No. Leave her be. Don't –

Tull Now off with that. And there's extra too for late return. You understand?

Pause.

You listening to me, miss? See, I in't mouse you thought I was. I makes the rules and you follow 'em. Now dress off and pay up cos I ain't hiring to you or your sisters no more.

Pause.

Must I take it from you? Well, if that's the way, I shall.

Princess Thass a man's anger, that is.

Tull No business of yours. This is me and customer.

Princess Found her wandering. She in't right. (*To* **Amy**.) Something's happened to you, in't it, my love?

Tull Turned thief. Thass what's happened.

She moves towards **Amy** *– smells her breath.*

Oh. Drunk are you? Well, seems to me, you can pay for the drink you can pay for the dress. Here, miss, here.

Princess   No. In't just drunk. There's something . . .

Tull and **Princess** *begin to remove* **Amy**'s *dress.*

Tull   What's this spoiling the cloth?

Tull *pulls away the dress to reveal the underskirt. It is drenched in blood.*

Amy   Blood wun't stop. Told me: pain, blood at first. But then it's over. But now won't stop. Just wanted it out of me. Make it stop.

Pause.

Tull   Dress off.

Princess   Mrs Tull –

Tull   Dress off.

Amy   Didn't want to be Mother.

Tull   So kill it? Reach up into your belly and rip it dead? Well, miss, it's pain eternal for you. That's Nature's cursing you, that's Lord cursing you and – yes –that's me cursing you too.

Amy   No. Dun't put that on me. Please.

Princess (*to* **Amy**)   Come, come. There's no curses here.

Tull   Oh, in't there? What I wun't have give to have my belly blow up like that –

Princess   Lost child didn't know what she did.

Tull   Well, dress is ruined now. Thass the stock spoiled.

Princess   Wash her up. Let her rest.

Tull   Dress off her and on her way.

Princess   Wash her, rest her. Thass what my heart says. And thass what I'm gonna do. (*To* **Amy**.) Thass it. You come with me.

Princess *starts to lead* **Amy** *to the rear of the shop.*

Tull (*to* **Princess**)   Where you going in my shop?

Princess   You say you wanted to be Mother. Can't be Mother when it's all stock and ledgers.

Tull   Thass . . . Mother looks after her own.

Princess   Mother dun't look on pain and confusion. Mother in't body and babies. Mother's in your acts.

Tull   Easy for you. Playing at Mother. But me. I'm in the real world. And thass hard. So – can't forgive. Can't forget. Gotta look to my stock.

Princess   There in't nothing of Mother in you. And maybe there never was.

Exit **Princess** *and* **Amy**.

Tull   Stephen? Stephen? You there?

Silence.

That world better than this one, Stephen?
Well, I bloody well hope so. Cos I want something better than this. And I bloody earned it. Stephen? Well, if that's the way of it, then I wanna little pleasure down here. Bloody great handfuls of Joy on Earth. Thass what I want.

Silence.

Stephen. Know you're bloody listening. Know you're bloody watching. So why don't you fucking well show yourself? STEPHEN! STEPHEN TULL, JUST YOU COME OUT HERE AND LISTEN TO ME!

Enter **Martin**.

Tull   Martin. Whatever are you wearing?

Pause. **Martin** *steps forward.*

Martin   Ain't Martin. It's Susan. Susan Guzzle. Mistress Susan Guzzle.

Tull   Oh, is it now?

Martin   And Susan's awful cross with her mother for being such a sad bitch when Susan needs her mother so.

Tull   And why does Susan need her mother?

Martin   Body's changing, Mother. Titties starting to grow. There's hair between my legs. And there's blood coming out of me. And I needs Mother to show me what to do.

Enter **Orme**.

Orme   And me too, Mother.

Tull   What's that?

Orme   Oh, Mother, don't you know your Kitty Fisher? The poorhouse and how they took me away from you? All me life I've been a searching and a searching and now I've found you. Oh, Mum, Mum.

He hugs **Tull**.

Tull   Martin – this is queer sport.

Martin   Ain't no Martin no more, Mum. Hanged hisself from a beam after breakfast. Says to me: Susan, tell the mistress I love her, but I can't stand this world no more. And I says: 'I shall', as the rope tightened round his neck.

Enter **Kedger** *and* **Philips**.

Philips   Oh, Mother, thought we'd lost you.

Tull   Oh, did you now?

Kedger   Oh, the world's an awful cruel place for tearing a family apart, in't it? But it's over now. Family's here.

Tull   Family?

The men all hold **Tull**.

Orme   Oooo – Ma. Thass good.

Tull   Lord. How many children I got?

Kedger   Oh, hundreds, Mother.

Tull   Well, ain't I been busy?

She pulls away.

Tull   What am I – ? Can't be playing these games. Come on, Martin. Thass enough games.

Martin   No. Playing's best thing we got. You wanna be Mother? Then – play.

Orme   Yes, Ma. Come play.

Tull   But . . .

Philips   All these years, Ma, with just your picture in my locket for company. Shipped off, cutting 'bacca in the sun 'til I thought me skin was gonna burn away. And stealing and saving and stealing and saving so I could pay the fare home, home to Mother.

Tull   No. In't playing. But . . .

Orme   Yeah?

Tull   Maybe . . . hiring. Thass something I could do. You wanna dress?

Philips   Oooo yes, ma.

Tull   And you?

Kedger   Yes, Ma.

Tull   Then let's get the measure of you.

Tull *starts to measure them. Enter* **Princess**.

Princess   What's this?

Tull   These are my customers, Princess. They're after hiring of dresses.

Princess   But . . . they're too big. They'll pull at the seams.

Tull   Then I'll have to stitch in extra.

Princess   But, Mrs Tull, men in dresses –

Tull   Said the kettle to the pot.

Princess   But that's different. I'm a character.

Tull   Oh no. Hundreds of 'em, in't that right?

Kedger   That's right.

Tull   And I shall hire to 'em. A shilling a dress a day. That's my price. Take it or leave it. Come on, Princess. You wanna work? Then lend a hand. See, I'm moving out of whores. Whores are finished and I'm moving into mollies.

Princess   But, Mrs Tull – these men are sodomites.

Tull   You're sure?

Princess   Every last one of them.

Tull   And what of it?

Princess   It in't right.

Tull   In't right? And who are you to judge?

Princess   It turns my stomach.

Tull   For that is the beauty of business. It judges no one. Let your churchman send your wretch to Hell, let your judge send him to Tyburn or the colonies. A businesswoman will never judge – if your money is good.

Princess   But sodomites –

Tull   And if your sodomite is a good customer, then that is where I shall do my business.

Princess   It in't natural.

Tull   Oh yes. I shall turn my head away when prick goes into arse. And I shall look to my purse. And all will be well. You wanna work? You want employment? Then come. I'm calling on you. Howdeedo, Princess, howdeedo. Now rig 'em.

Orme   Ma. Can we have a house?

Tull   For all the mollies?

Orme   For all the mollies.

Tull   Oh yes. Thass it. Molly house. Come, Princess. Rig and pay. Rig and pay. Molly house is open for business.

Princess   Mrs Tull –

Tull   Oh no. In't Tull no more. Tull's dead and buried see. From this day on all shall call me Mother.

More **Mollies** *appear.*

'End of Act One'

Mollies
   Rejoice!
   A home at last
   Mother is here now
   Sorrow is past
   Sorrow's past past past!

   Rejoice!
   We'll live in light
   Our bodies are ours now
   Hearts are our own now
   Our choice
   Our promised land.
   Rejoice! Rejoice!

God *and* **Eros** *appear.*

All
   Reconciled, reconciled!
   God and Eros reconciled!

Pleasure in profit
Profit in pleasure
God and Eros reconciled!

God
Morality is history
Now profit reigns supreme

Eros
And love can speak its name out loud
Now business loves a queen

All
We are the future
We are the light
This is our time
This our right

This is our Happy End
But this is just the start
This is a marriage
Of purse and arse and heart

God bless us one and all tonight
Let us live in Heaven's light
We're sure that what we do is right
So shit on all those who call this sodomy
Shit on those who call this sodomy
Shit on those who call this sodomy
We call it fabulous.

Act Two

Scene Six

2001. A loft apartment. **Josh**, **Charlie** *and* **Tina**. **Tina***'s face is covered in piercings.*

Charlie   Do you know what I call her?

Josh   No. No, I don't.

Charlie   Tell him.

Tina   No.

Charlie   Go on. Tell him what I call you.

Tina   The Iron Lady.

Charlie   It's fucking incredible. Another day, another piercing. Every time I come home she's done another one. Fucking blood everywhere. And I goes to her – for fuck's sake clean yourself up. Cos I in't doing it again. In't that right?

Tina   Yeah, that's right.

Josh   Absolutely. Have you got the – ?

Charlie   She's got fucking hundreds of 'em. I don't understand it. Why d'you do that to yourself?

Tina   I dunno.

Charlie   I mean, I give her anything she wants. But – oh no. Daytime telly, piercings. Thass her life.

Josh   Well, whatever turns you on.

Charlie   Yesterday I come home, she's got the mirror on the floor and she's stood over it – starkers – blood –drip, drip, drip – and she's doing her . . . whassis . . . her . . .

Tina   Labia.

Charlie   Thass it. Doing her labia.

Josh   Really?

Charlie   I had a right go at her. But she won't stop. I think she's disturbed.

Tina   No. Just –

Charlie   Yes you are. Total fucking headcase.

Tina   Don't you talk to me like that, you fucking –

Josh   Actually, I've got a few. Piercings.

Charlie   Yeah?

Josh   Yuh. Tits. Knob. Just not the face, you know. Work. Have you got the coke?

Charlie   I want to have kids.

Tina   Don't.

Charlie   Be great, couple of kids.

Tina   Says you.

Charlie   Thass why I deal, right? Put a bit by so we can bring 'em up. Move to the country, I reckon.

Tina   I don't like the country.

Josh   I could really do with a line.

Charlie   But I mean, how the fuck is she gonna have a kid? Poor fucker would have to fight through half a ton of ironwork just to get out of her.

Tina   Oh, fuck off.

Charlie   And she couldn't feed it. There's more metal than nipple.

Tina   Why do you always do that? / Why do you always put me down like that?

Charlie   I'm just saying, I'm just telling him, that's all, babe.

Tina   Well, don't. / Cos I don't want to hear it, alright?

Charlie   Just having a laugh. If you can't take a joke.

Tina   Oh, fuck off. Fuck off.

Josh   Hey. Hey. Hey. Listen. Listen. Have you got the coke?

Charlie   Special delivery.

He produces a large bag of coke.

Quality.

Enter Will, carrying a video cassette.

Will   Oh hi. Dropping off supplies? Fabulous. I thought we had enough for a week and then these silly queens came over for supper and – hoover, hoover – you would have thought Colombia was about to fall into the fucking ocean.

Charlie   Having a bit of a party, are yer?

Josh   Something like that.

Will   More of an orgy really.

Charlie   Right.

Will   Well, a sex party.

Josh   A sex-party-orgy-underwear sort of thing.

Tina   Uuugh.

Josh   Sorry?

Tina   I said: Uuuugh.

Charlie   Don't worry about her. She's just a bit – Whass the word?

Tina   Homophobic.

Charlie   She dun't like poofs. But I tell her: poofs, they got it sorted.

Will   Is that right?

Will puts the video into the machine.

Charlie   Not like before, is it? Now it's your poofs know how to enjoy themselves, it's your poofs with the money nowadays. Poofs running the country now, in't there? Do all my business with the poofs. Well, you don't get the hassle, do you? (*To* **Tina**.) Poofs paying for your piercings, that is.

Will presses play. A porn video plays.

Tina   Uuuugggh.

Charlie   Fucking hell. He's going for it with that fist, in't he?

Josh   Oh, I met that one once.

Charlie   What the one with his −?

Josh   Yes. At a party in Chicago. I would have slept with him only I had a flight the next morning and he had to get up early for church.

Doorbell rings. Exit **Josh**.

Charlie   I wanted to try all that stuff. Gang-bang stuff. Took her up this fetish club, didn't I?

Tina   Yeah.

Charlie   Told her: I'm not getting pissed on or nothing but . . . She didn't like it. Said it was −

Tina   Boring.

Charlie   That's the trouble with her, see.

Will   Ennui.

Charlie   No. She gets bored easily.

Enter **Josh** *and* **Tom**.

Josh   You're very early.

Tom   I know, sorry. It's just I don't know the area so I left a lot of time. But actually it's really easy to find, isn't it? If you want me to go away and come back –

Josh   No, no.

Tom   This is really nice. Like in a magazine, isn't it?

Josh   That depends what magazines you read.

Tom   Yeah, right, right. (*Sees* **Tina**.) Oh. Is there gonna be women? Only I –

Charlie   No, mate, you're alright. We're pissing off.

Josh   I'll get your money.

Exit **Josh**.

Tom (*to* **Tina**)   Sorry. Was that rude? I didn't mean to be rude. I really like your . . . your . . . (*piercings*).

Tina   Fuck off.

Tom   Yeah, right. Right. Sorry. I'm probably talking too much. I just did a couple of E. I always feel better. New people, new situations an E. Because naturally I'm sort of introverted but with an E . . .

Charlie   It's legs in the air and off you go, you dirty slag.

Tom   Yeah, right. I'm wild. Up for it at compuserve dot com. That's my address. Which gets me quite a lot of attention actually. Oooo – is that charlie?

Will   Would you like some?

Tom   Can I? Ooo, I'm mad for the charlie, me.

He opens the bag and rubs the coke on his gums.

Oh, that's good. Bit of charlie's good after a couple of E, isn't it? Cos sometimes with the E . . . Well, I find it hard to connect with people so I take the E and I connect with them and I go to bed with them and I can't always perform. You know. Which is the downside of E. I mean, not always.

Well, not all that often actually. Often I go like a train. That's what they say. Loads of blokes say that to me. Just sometimes . . . Did you know you're bleeding?

Tina   Wassat?

Tom   You've got blood down your leg.

Tina   Oh. Right.

Charlie   Fucking hell, I told you. Pierced her . . . wassis . . .

Tina   Labia.

Charlie   And now it wun't stop. Clean yourself up. Where's your bathroom?

Will   Here. Let me show you.

Tina   Come and help us.

Charlie   Fucking headcase.

Exit **Will***,* **Tina** *and* **Charlie***.* **Tom** *takes more coke. Produces a bottle of water. Does another E. Doorbell rings.*

Tom   Excuse me. Excuse me. Your –

Doorbell rings. Exit **Tom***. Re-enters followed by* **Edward** *and* **Phil***.* **Phil** *carries a large bag.*

Edward   Hi. Edward. Phil. Sorry, we're so early. But the roads were clear and – Gosh. Quite a place you've got here.

Tom   Oh, it's not actually my –

Edward   Brought along some toys. Hope you don't mind. Phil.

Phil *hands* **Tom** *the bag.* **Tom** *unzips the bag.*

Edward   Quite a collection we've got, haven't we, Phil?

Tom *pulls an enormous dildo out of the bag.*

Edward   Dildos, butt plugs, et cetera. Always like to give them an airing, don't we, Phil?

Phil Yeah.

Edward We go to quite a lot of these things. We're old hands so to speak. Always worth travelling for a good bit of action. Isn't that right, Phil?

Phil Oh yeah.

Edward *produces a video camera.*

Edward No objection to the camera, I hope?

Tom Oh no, no.

Edward There's always a shy one of course but I have to say most people find it an enormous turn-on, don't they, Phil?

Phil Yeah.

Edward Hoping to add a little watersports to the collection this evening actually. Do you . . . ?

Tom No.

Edward Pity. Right then.

He produces a very complicated harness from the bag.

Now then. How's about I slip into something a little less comfortable?

Tom Oh yeah.

Edward Through here? Super.

Exit **Edward** *with harness.*

Phil Sorry about him. He dominates, doesn't he?

Tom That's alright.

Phil Watch out if you fuck him. Back-seat driver. Up a bit, down a bit. Faster. Slower. I have to gag him.

Tom Yeah?

Phil He's grateful for it really.

Enter **Edward**, *half-undressed.*

Edward   Phil. I'm gonna need a hand.

Phil   In a minute.

Exit **Edward**.

You been to one of these before?

Tom   Well, sort of . . . well, no. No I haven't. Exciting,
isn't it?

Phil   Is it?

Tom   I think so. Really, really exciting. Because actually,
you know, I only came out recently. You know, when I
moved to London. Two months and I've like totally
changed. Like: there's Old Me and New Me.

Phil   Is that right?

Tom   Oh yeah. And Old Me was like . . . stop me if I'm
talking shit, alright? Sometimes on the E, I . . .

Phil   Alright.

Tom   Well, I know this is mad but I feel like Old Me was
living in the Olden Days. History and that. Really, really
old-fashioned. All scared and no sex and no drugs. And now
there's New Me – and I'm like totally Today. I'm Now. Do
you know what I mean?

Phil   Oh yeah.

Tom   Time machine. Two months and I've travelled
hundreds of years into the future. Only the future's like now.
I mean, look at me. Clubs. E. Shagging all sorts of blokes.
It's great. And now this.

Enter **Edward**, *wrestling with the harness.*

Edward   Phil.

Phil   Coming.

Exit **Edward**.

Tom My first actual live-sex party. Fucking great, isn't it?

Phil Yeah. Great.

Enter **Charlie**, **Tina**, **Josh** *and* **Will**. **Tina** *is bleeding badly.*
Charlie *has a towel covered in blood.*

Tina Get your fucking hands off me. / I don't want to be
touched.

Charlie Just trying to clean you up, thass all.

Tina I can't stand you touching me. / I hate that.

Josh Hey, hey, come on, come on. / Let's just cool it.

Will Watch where you're going. Blood on the − hey. Not
the sofa.

Charlie Come on, babes. Let's clean you up.

Tina I'm alright. I'm alright.

Tina *goes to sit on the sofa.*

Will Not the sofa. Not on the sofa.

Tina Just leave me alone.

Tina *is just about to bleed on the sofa.* **Will** *pulls her away from the
sofa.*

Will No!

Tina Get your hands off me. You fucking poof! I hate
you. I hate you all. I hate your money. I hate your big
houses. And I hate your fucking sofas. Fucking sticking your
fists up each other. Fucking disgusting. / Fucking sick.

Will Alright, that's enough. / Because actually now, I'm
getting really offended.

Tina Oh, is it? Oh, is it really? Come on then, let's have
yer.

Tina *puts up her fists and goes to fight* **Will**. *Suddenly, she faints.*
Charlie *catches her.*

Charlie   Lie her down.

Josh *picks up* **Tina**'s *legs.* **Charlie** *starts to move them towards the sofa.*

Will   No. No. Not the sofa. Through here.

Will *leads the way as* **Josh** *and* **Charlie** *carry* **Tina** *off to the bedroom. As they do,* **Edward** *enters. He is now almost into the harness and is wearing a leather-studded jockstrap with motorcycle boots.*

Edward   Phil, I really need you to –

Phil   Yeah, yeah.

Exit **Phil** *and* **Edward**.

Tina   What happened?

Charlie   It's alright, babe. Everything's going to be alright.

Exit **Will** *and* **Charlie** *and* **Josh**, *carrying* **Tina**. **Tom** *stands lost. Enter* **Eros**.

'Phoebus Reprise'

Eros
Feel Eros chasing through your veins
Through heart and head and skin
This feeling's all, this chemistry
So let the game begin.

Tom   Wow. You're beautiful.

Eros
Let Eros still the hand of time
May youth be ever yours
With age comes grief but youth is free
So play and leave remorse.

Eros *takes* **Tom**'s *hand, sings him a song. As he does so,* **Will** *and* **Josh**'s *flat melts away and becomes the molly house.* **Mollies** *swarm around* **Tom** *and* **Eros**.

Tom   This is really, really exciting.

Eros
  Come play, come play
  Up up and play
  And playing dream of me
  And playing dream, playing dream
  And playing dream of me.

Scene Seven

The molly house. Four **Mollies** *– whooping and goosing each other. Enter* **Princess**.

Princess   No no no. (*To one* **Molly**.) See, you must take extra care with this 'un. This is for gliding. You can't go rushing about in this one. You must – like this.

He glides. The **Mollies** *giggle.*

(*To another* **Molly**.)   And you, miss. Got my eye on you. Prancing about after paramours, lifting them skirts. That in't right. Dressed up fine and fine you must be.

Mollies *giggle.*

Princess   Oooo, but you mollies is silly creatures. If it weren't for her I wouldn't stick this.

Mollies *giggle.*

Princess   In't one of you understands how to carry a dress. If all you want's a jig and a fuck then why rig up as woman, eh?

Enter **Tull**.

Tull   Here she is. Here's Mother.

Mollies *rush to* **Tull***, kiss her hands.*

Tull   Thass it. Welcome. Well and in't the Princess rigged you fine? Gonna be a good night tonight. Best night ever at Mother's.

Mollies *cheer.*

Tull   Now, my dears, beer waiting for you through there. Some of your sisters already here. And more to come. Dancing'll start soon. So go on – off you skip.

Exit **Mollies**.

Princess   How did you find him?

Tull   Very low, Princess. Lower un low.

Princess   Thass what I thought.

Tull   'Oh, Mother,' says he. 'In't I been foolish. Thought Kitty Fisher loved me.'

Princess   Can't trust your molly. Didn't I say?

Tull   And I says: 'Susan, love, I'm sure he does love you. Just it comes out peculiar.'

Princess   I should say it does. Fucking any man or boy that comes in here.

Tull   Oh no. It in't bad as that.

Princess   Bad as that an more. Last night alone saw him a-petting and a-bundling with three of 'em severally and then – jug of beer later – three of 'em together. Can't get badder than that.

Tull   Thass youth.

Princess   Thass wickedness. Thass the sodomite way. Fuck 'em once and then find another.

Tull   But I'm sure in my heart Kitty loves his Susan Guzzle still.

Princess   That sort dun't know love.

Tull   Them too – true love.

Princess And how can you tell?

Tull Mother's instincts. You seen Kitty?

Princess Mrs Tull –

Tull What's that? Still harping on Tull? Ain't heard that in a while.

Princess Well and maybe you should. See, these games –

Tull No. Don't pull me back to Tull, love. Mother now and I in't never been happier. Now, see, I got a plan. Win Kitty back for Susan. You watch. Tonight's the night for Mother's plan. And once tonight is done – Kitty and Susan's gonna be reconciled. Got Susan ready now all I gotta do's find Kitty and –

Princess You know what they call you, your mollies?

Tull What's that?

Princess Clap.

Tull Thass just one of their names.

Princess Mother Clap.

Tull And where's the harm in that? If it makes 'em happy then Mother Clap I shall be. You seen Kitty?

Enter **Kedger**, **Philips** *and* **Lawrence**. *They are all in men's clothes.*

Tull Well – what have we here?

Kedger Customer for you Mother.

Tull Well, in't you a fine un? In't he a fine un?

Philips Found him up Moorfields.

Tull Oh, nothing up Moorfields nowadays. Well, nothing but the poxed and prickless. So come and welcome to Mother's.

Lawrence Right. Howdo.

Tull   Thass a shilling in.

Lawrence   Right.

Lawrence *gives her a shilling.*

Tull (*calls*)   Ned! Customer! And a shilling for the dress.

Lawrence   The dress?

Tull   Thass right. Princess and Ned'll dress you.

Lawrence   But I don't –

Tull   Oh, all wear dresses here. In't that right?

Philips   Thass right.

Lawrence   But I in't the type.

Enter **Amy** *dressed as a man, carrying a dress.*

Lawrence   What's that?

Tull   Thass Ned.

Lawrence   That a lad?

Tull   Lad now in't you, my love?

Amy   Thass right.

Tull   Didn't have much of a time of it as Woman, did you, Ned?

Amy   Thass right.

Tull   Did awful wicked deed as Woman. Sent infant, wun't you? New life growing inside Woman here. And she ripped it out and bled and bled. But I found it in my heart to forgive. And since Ned chopped at his hair and slipped into his breeches he's been a great help. Although his temper's awful fierce – so mind him. Now. What's your molly name, my dear?

Lawrence   How do you mean?

Tull All have names at Mother's. China Mary, Primrose Mary, Garter Mary, Orange Mary, Pomegranate Moll. Young Fish Hannah, Old Fish Hannah, Miss Selina, Kitty Fisher, Kitty Cambric. Flying Horse Moll, Thumbs and Elbows Jenny, Hardware Nan –

Lawrence Susan.

Tull Oh no. For we already have our own Susan Guzzle. So let's . . .

Philips The Mistress Girl of Midriff.

Tull Oh yes, lovely.

Enter **Orme** *in a dress, watches.*

Tull Right, Princess, Ned, off with the Mistress Girl and rig her.

Philips And us too, Mother.

Tull Course. And you too. Rig 'em all.

Exit **Philips, Kedger, Princess, Lawrence** *and* **Amy.**

Orme Well and in't he a fine un? I shall be offering a curtsey and a 'Will you dance?' to that one tonight.

Tull What? And no thought of your Susan?

Orme Course. Always a thought for Susan.

Tull Susan'll be thinking of you. Loves you bad.

Orme And I love Susan.

Tull You sure of that?

Orme And I shall come back to Susan. Just – we must fuck who we will. Else what's the point of a molly house? Might as well be Man and Wife like rest of the world. 'Go on, Susan,' I say. 'Have another. Have a score. I'll love you all the more.' But silly girl just moons it about and waits and waits. Thass Patient Griselda not my Susan Guzzle.

Tull You was happy enough to play the marrying game.

Orme   And that was lovely, Ma, and you married us good but then . . . Oh, Ma, I get bored so easy. Do you think that's bad? Am I a bad un?

Tull   No, love. In't none of Mother's children bad. I in't here to judge. Just got to find a way so you're happy and Susan's happy.

Orme   But how?

Tull   Ah, well . . .

Orme   Ask me, happiness is like Fortune's wheel. One's up, t'other's down.

Tull   No. I got a plan. New game. Bring you and Susan together. You wanna play?

Orme   What game's that?

Tull   You shall see. You must wear this so (*gives* **Orme** *a blindfold*) and wait in the next room and we will fetch you when all is ready. Will you play along?

Orme   Is it a good game, Ma?

Tull   It's a marvel.

Orme   Then I shall.

Exit **Orme**.

Tull   Susan! Susan!

Enter **Martin** *in a dress.*

Tull   Susan. You better get yourself ready.

Martin   There in't no point, Ma.

Tull   Well, thass where you're wrong.

Martin   I lost him, Ma, and that's that, gotta face facts.

Tull   You dun't want to give up that easy, girl. You love him?

Martin   I hurt all the time. Is that love?

Tull   Thass a part of it. Gonna win him back you see. You trust your ma?

Martin   Course.

Tull   Then do as Mother says cos new game's about to begin.

Enter **Lawrence, Kedger** *and* **Philips**, *now dressed as mollies, and* **Princess**.

Philips   Well, in't she a pretty miss?

Tull   Oh yes, Mistress Girl. Thass lovely.

Lawrence   I feel foolish.

Tull   Well, you looks a picture.

Sound of **Mollies** *within.*

Ooo, dancing's about to begin.

Exit **Martin. Mollies** *enter, including several musicians. The* **Mollies** *dance.*

'Mother Clap's Maggot'

Mollies
    Whoever the fuck wants to fuck me, fuck me
    Cos you are the finest, the finest I've fucked.
    Whoever is lying beside me, sighing
    Whoever is coming inside me, dying
    The stranger the stranger I'm fucking the better
    But closing my eyes and I still see your face
    So we'll fuck til the day when we're finally fucked
    Til we lie in the sod, til we rot
    And we'll smile at the worms as they gnaw at our flesh
    And tell them how finely we fucked.

Tull   The words you use – enough to make a body burn with shame. (*To* **Orme**.) Now you – blindfold on and into the next room.

Exit **Orme**.

Tull   Welcome, welcome one and all to Mother Clap's Molly House.

Princess   No, you don't wanna –

Tull   Knows what they call me, Princess. An I like it. Mother Clap. Thass me.

Tonight rules is left at the door. What do you wanna be today? Maid or man? You decide. Husband or wife? You choose. Ravished or ravisher. Thass for you to say. Cos there in't no bugger here gonna tell you what to be.

And if you wanna take your paramour in private, take 'em to a room, lock the door and find your pleasure there, then Ma says: Good. And here's the key.

She holds up a key.

And I don't charge much. But I am a woman of business. And if anyone says I in't paying I says – I says it sweetly and I says it with love – but I says: Bugger off.

Now tonight. Tonight's a special night. Cos now we got a game like one that in't ever been. Cos tonight our Susan Guzzle – well, let's call Susan Guzzle forth. Music there.

'Birthing Scene'

*Musicians play as **Tull** recites.*

Susan, Susan, in't the time to hideaway
Susan, Susan, Mother dear
Says: Show yourself and say
'How doo' to all your sisters gathered here.

*Enter **Martin**. He has a pregnant stomach.*

Tull   Oh, Susan – what's this? A belly chuck?

Martin   Thass right, Ma. Up and up it blew.

Tull
Oh, Susan, in't this wond'rous luck?
Oh, Susan, Mother's proud of you.

Martin

    An' shall I have to wait for month on month
    Before an infant peeps from out me cunt?

Tull

    Oh no, my love. Ma's art shall do its work on you
    Right here and now is when the infant's due.
    But labour's hard – you know the pain is great.

Martin   Oh, pain, Ma, don't know if –

Tull

                     But wait!
    Let's bring the father forth. He'll see you through.
    The love of one who's good and true
    Means we can bear life's pain and suffering.
    The father there and let the birth begin.

More music – fuller and louder. Two **Mollies** *exit. Re-enter with*
Orme *blindfolded.*

Tull   Kitty Fisher – are you listening?

Orme (*laughs*)   Yes, Ma.

Tull

    Kitty – glad tidings of great joy I bring to Earth.
    You ever heard of how a virgin once gave birth?

Orme   Yes, Ma.

Tull

    Well, tonight there's something queerer yet
    Unmask him there and let
    Our Kitty wonder at the sight.

Orme's *blindfold is removed.*

Orme   Susan!

Tull

    Come womb – the time is right
    Let waters break, our Susan's due

Come precious child
Ma waits, world waits, love waits for you.

The molly musicians play a beautiful slow piece as **Martin**'s *labour progresses. Finally, silence as the baby – a wooden doll – is pulled out from* **Martin**'s *skirts.* **Tull** *lifts the baby up to the Heavens – then slaps the baby's bottom.*

Mollies   Waaagh.

Tull *hands the baby to* **Martin.**

Orme   Susan. What is this?

Martin   Infant love. Mine and yours. Come see.

Orme   But I dun't want infant.

Martin   Look, that's your eyes. My nose. Our mouth.
Come, love.

Orme   Thass a stupid game. You told me –

Tull   Oh yes. Thass a very pretty child. Thass lovely,
Susan. Come on, Kitty.

Orme   I in't playing that. That's stupid. Seems to me you
better let me choose the games now on. Who wants a dance
there? Come. Let's dance.

Tull   Just you hold baby in your arms.

Orme   Oh no. Didn't want molly house so it could all be
marrying and babies. (*To* **Martin.**) Sorry, love. But there
in't no pleasure in that. (*To* **Lawrence.**) Will you dance
with me, sir?

Lawrence   I in't much of a dancer.

Orme   I shall show you the way. There in't much to a jig.
Soon have you jigging. Come, sisters. Away and dance.

Exit all but **Tull, Martin** *and* **Princess.** *We can hear the*
Mollies, *off, dancing and singing during the following.*

Martin   You ruined it all now, in't you?

Tull Susan, love –

Martin Lost him now.

Tull No.

Martin Don't think I don't see it, cos I do. Baby? Thass not what I want. Baby – thass you. Thass you're wanting. Can't make me into what you want to be. Cos that goes nowhere. I don't want this. Want him. And he's gone for ever.

*Exit **Martin**, leaving baby.*

Tull Oh, Princess. What am I to do?

Princess Mrs Tull. I'm a man. Man's feelings. And I wanna tell yer –

Tull What's that?

Princess What a man likes is to be around a woman. A woman of life and vigour. A woman worth watching. Mrs Tull, I've been watching you.

Tull Oh, have you now?

Princess Do you think that's bad – man watching you?

Tull Oh no. I like that. But you're . . .

Princess A man. A man's feelings. Oh, let me show you.

Tull I got money to count.

Princess Husband's dead. You gotta kiss the living.

Tull No. I don't want to do that.

She moves to exit, turns.

What would I be kissing? Man, woman or hermaphrodite?

Princess Close your eyes.

Tull Yes?

Princess   Close your eyes and see what pictures come into your head. Alright?

Tull   Alright.

Princess *kisses her.*

Princess   What do you see now?

Tull   Man. (*He kisses her neck.*). Woman. (*He kisses her breasts.*) Hermaphrodite.

Princess   And which do you want?

Tull   Oh, Princess –

Princess   See, Mrs Tull, I'll be anything for you. Just tell me what you want me to be and that's what I'll make myself. I'm a blank and you can choose. Ain't no dignity in it, is there? I know that. Where's his dignity? you're saying. Well, I say: bugger dignity and bugger pride. Cos what's pride when love comes a-calling? And thass what I got for you, Mrs Tull – love.

Tull   Princess –

Princess   So come – what's it to be? What do you want?

Tull   I want . . . I want . . . I want what my dry old body in't never gonna give me, that's what I want. I want life inside me – here. You gonna give me that? No, you in't. Ain't nothing gonna make this live. In't no game gonna make that good.

Princess   I in't playing a game.

Tull   Oh, it's all games here. Mother Clap? Thass a game. Princess? Game? We're all playing, in't we? Best we'll ever have. So, come my mollies. Mollies – come.

Enter men in their underwear, including **Phil** *and* **Josh**.

Tull (*to* **Phil**)   You wanna take your paramour? Then come take him, take him.

Princess   Mrs Tull –

Tull   The sodomites are here, Princess. Sodomy's arrived. You wanna look aside? Turns you stomach still, dun't it? But it's pleasure to them and that's enough for me.

Princess   I can't stay for this. I'm going now. Packing up and going see? Tell me stay, Mrs Tull. Love you. Love you. Alright. Last you'll see of me. Thass goodbye for ever now.

Exit **Princess**. **Phil** *starts to fuck* **Josh**.

Tull   That's it. Go on. That's it. Pleasure 'til morning comes. Pleasure 'til Judgement day. Oh yes. Pleasure, pleasure, pleasure. Pleasure ever more.

Scene Eight

2001. Loft apartment. The party is in full swing. Music playing. Various men wander through in their underwear. **Phil** *is fucking* **Josh** *over the sofa.* **Josh** *sniffs from a bottle of poppers. There is a porn video playing.*

'Pleasure'

Eros
   Pleasure pleasure pleasure's here.
   You wanna touch me? I gotta think about that.
   You wanna take me? OK.
   You wanna have a good time?
   Come on come on come on.

   You got the sweetest booty of any boy in town
   I love that booty booty and I am going down
   And down down down

   Shake it take it don't fake it
   Make it real sister
   Go sister, you're such a ho sister on video sister
   Make me sing Miss Thing
   With your ring a ling a ling a ling

Tomorrow's never coming
And yesterday is gone
Now is how I wanna be
So bring the pleasure on
And on and on and on

Phil   How you doing?

Josh   Yeah. Great.

More fucking. Enter **Charlie** *from bedroom, carrying the bloody towel. He calls back to* **Tina***.*

Charlie   Just – lie still. Keep pressing on it. You're gonna be alright.

He sees **Josh** *and* **Phil***.*

Alright?

Exit **Charlie** *to the bathroom.* **Phil** *uses the remote to rewind the video.*

Enter **Edward** *with the camcorder. He videos them.*

Edward   Oh yes. Always like to get the highlights on the camcorder, don't we, Phil?

Phil   Yeah.

More fucking. **Edward** *continues videoing.*

Edward   I've become rather good at this. And now, of course, you can get these fantastic editing packages. Many a merry evening I spend editing my footage of Phil. Off you go, I say to him. Off you go and have your fun. Bit of sleazy slut action for you. Because I've got you right here with me on tape.

Josh   I'm sorry, I –

Josh *pulls away from* **Phil***.*

Edward   Whoops. Hope I didn't throw you.

Josh   No. It's not that.

Edward   There's always a shy one.

Josh   Oh no. The camera's fine.

Two men cross the stage and exit.

Edward   Hello. I think the action's just about to shift to the bathroom.

*Exit **Edward**. Enter **Charlie** from bathroom. Enter **Will** from kitchen.*

Charlie   You got any more towels?

Will   What?

Charlie   You got any clean towels? (*To **Phil** and **Josh**.*) Sorry about this, lads. (*To **Will**.*) Only she's still bleeding. Won't stop.

Will   I'll have a look.

Charlie   Cheers.

*He gives **Will** the bloody towel. Exit **Will**. **Charlie** stands awkwardly watching **Phil** and **Josh** fucking.*

I try and understand her. I really do. Every other bloke she's been with has knocked her about. All I've ever done is buy her whatever she wanted but still she . . . The only time she's happy is after she's done a piercing. Then next day she's all moody again and she starts planning the next one. I mean, what's it all about?

*Enter **Will** with towels.*

Will   Here.

Charlie   Thanks, mate.

*Exit **Charlie** to bedroom.*

Will (*to **Josh***)   Look. I think maybe we should cover the sofa.

Josh   The sofa's fine.

Will   Just, you know . . . stains.

Josh   I'll be careful.

Will   Well, just make sure you do.

Enter **Edward** *from bathroom.*

Edward   Phil. Quick. There's rimming.

Phil   In a minute.

Exit **Will** *to kitchen.*

Edward   But it might be over / in a minute.

Phil   I'm busy.

Edward   Honestly, I've driven us all the way up here. / I think the least you —

Phil   I drove us up here.

Edward   — can do — I thought you liked rimming.

Phil   Yeah, well.

Edward   Really, sometimes I just don't understand you.

Exit **Edward**. **Josh** *pulls away from* **Phil** *and sits on the sofa.*

Phil   Sorry about him. He's always like that. But you get used to it.

Josh   Yeah, right.

Phil   I say I'm gonna leave him. But I never do. He's positive.

Josh   Right.

Phil   And, well, you don't like to leave them when they're at death's door, do you?

Josh   He doesn't seem like —

Phil   A few years ago he was like this little old stick man. I had to feed him, clean him up. And then these new medicines come along and now look at him, running around like a fucking kid. I could move on but I'm sort of stuck with him now. It's alright. We have a laugh. Do you wanna have another go?

Josh   No. Thank you.

Phil   Right. Well, I better go and check on him.

Exit **Phil** *to bathroom. Enter* **Will** *from kitchen.*

Will   What? Finished already?

Josh   Just . . . coming up for air.

Will   And how was he?

Josh   Fabulous. Yeah. Fantastic fuck. And you?

Will   Me? Oh, you know.

Josh   Had anyone fabulous yet?

Will   No. Not yet.

Josh   Well, you wanna get in there.

Will   Yeah, right. Listen –

Enter **Tom**.

Tom   Great party. Really, really great.

Josh   Here we go. Just your type.

Will   No. Not really. Listen. I don't want to –

Josh   Good luck. (*Hands* **Tom** *the poppers.*) Here. You might need these.

Tom   Oh, right. Triffic. Right.

Exit **Josh**. *Pause.*

Tom   Hello.

Will   Hello.

Pause.

Tom   I think you're really attractive.

Will   Thank you.

Pause.

Tom   I hope you don't mind me saying that.

Will   Not at all.

Pause.

Tom   Is he your boyfriend? Josh?

Will   God, that's a difficult question.

Tom   Is it? Sorry.

Will   Oh, it's just so fucking complicated.

Tom   Right.

Will   I mean, we don't fuck any more. Haven't fucked in years.

Tom   I see.

Will   Although sometimes we still do threesomes together if we're in the mood.

Tom   Got you.

Will   But not very often. But we live together. Joint mortgage and all that. And I care about him. Whatever you'd call that feeling.

Tom   Love.

Will   That kind of thing. And he's always meeting people. German boys or Portuguese boys – a Japanese once – and he's always going to live in Hamburg or Aporto or a little place outside Hiroshima – because this time it really is love and he's leaving and all of that. But it never happens.

Tom   Right. Right.

Tom *moves to kiss* **Will**.

Will   Listen. I'm sorry. But you're not my type.

Tom   Oh, I see. So – what is your type?

Will   Oh, I don't know. I forgot a long time ago. (*Indicates porn.*) Well, I suppose that's my type. Until you actually meet them. And then they open their mouth and it's a total turn-off. Look, if you want to suck me off.

Tom   Alright then.

Will   Maybe something will happen.

Tom *starts to suck* **Will** *off. Enter* **Edward**, *with the camcorder.*

Edward   Oh yes. I feel like chicken tonight.

Tom *goes to move.*

Will   No. Don't stop. Don't stop!

Several more men come in.

That's it. That's good. Come on, everyone. Come and look. We're having fun in here. Oh yes. We're having a fucking fantastic time here.

Tom *tries to pull away but* **Will** *pushes him down and holds his head hard.*

Will   I told you not to stop. Good boy. Good boy. That's good.

Tom *chokes.*

Will   Take it all. Take all of it. Who else wants to join in? Why not everyone? Yeah, come on. Everyone join in.

Tom   No.

He pushes **Will** *off.*

I was really looking forward to this evening. This is all I ever wanted. All them years stuck at home listening to me dad: Fucking poofs this, fucking queers that. And I thought: You're history, you. Cos I'm a poof, but I in't telling you. Oh no. One day I'm just gonna up and go. Stick a note on the fridge. 'Fuck the family.' Little husband with his little wife and their little kids. That's history. And I'm the future. This is the future. People doing what they want to do. People being who they want to be. So why . . . ? Why do you have to make it wrong?

Exit **Tom**.

Edward   Do you know, I think I might edit that bit out.

Phil   No. Leave it in. Be good for a laugh.

Edward   Think so? Possibly. Right then. I still haven't got any watersports. Who's going to oblige?

Enter **Charlie**.

Charlie   Listen, lads. Sorry, I don't wanna . . . but she's . . . oh fuck. Sorry, lads. But she's not breathing. Can someone . . . ?

Pause.

Lads. We gotta do something.

Scene Nine

Amelia, **Cranton**, **Bolton** *and the other whores pray.*

'The Whores' Prayer'

Whores
  Father, look down on your children now the customers
    have gone.
  Father look down on our brothel empty – how shall we
    carry on?
  Ev'ry man's turned molly and ev'ry maid's alone
  Father – bring them back from Sodom, bring the buggers
    home.

Bolton   Waste of time you ask me.

Amelia   On your knees, miss, mouth as wide as you can and – up to the Heavens.

Whores
Father fill your brothels 'til they're brimming, show us joy
once more
Father don't abandon me, or me, or me – an honest
simple whore
Father – world'll soon be empty if ev'ry man's turned
queer
Father – man must lie with maid again – oh bring
the buggers here.

Cranton   Well – and much good may that do us.

Amelia   Oh, he's listening, miss, and any day now he'll
send us a sign.

The molly house. **Tull** *is counting the money. Enter* **Lawrence**.

Lawrence   Scuse me. I dun't want to be a bother. But
they're all doing it. In public.

Tull   Wait, love. Ma's . . . ten, eleven, twelve . . .

Lawrence   I don't think that's right.

Tull   Well, each finds his own pleasure here.

Lawrence   I mean, Moorfields, thass dark. You get the
odd fumbler when you're in the act – but I push 'em away. I
like to take 'em one at a time.

Tull (*writing in book*)   Twenty-three, twenty-four, twenty-
five.

Lawrence   See, there's still right and wrong, in't there?
And I say: I'm man and I take 'em and thass right. And I
don't watch others and others dun't watch me. Cos thass
wrong. But this lot . . . candles a-blazing, great piles of 'em.
I think that's very wrong.

Tull   Thass how they like it. Thirty, thirty-one, thirty-two.

Lawrence   Well, thass not as I like it. Can I have a key?

Tull   Wassat, love?

Lawrence   For a room.

Tull   Well . . .

Lawrence   I have my shilling. See. Thass my last shilling but I wanna . . . paramour in private, as you said.

Tull   Yes, I said, love, but see . . .

Lawrence   My money's good.

Tull   But see, love, Kitty Fisher – oh, I know Kitty Fisher gives it strong with a fine un like you and course you wants to take Kitty – and Lord knows there's plenty of 'em has had Kitty – but see thing is Kitty –

Lawrence   It in't Kitty.

Tull   No?

Lawrence   No. That in't my type. I know that type – it's all fine words and fancy games with that type, in't it?

Tull   Oh yes. Kitty plays awful games.

Lawrence   And that in't the type to – oh, I in't never spoke to woman like this before.

Tull   Oh, I in't woman, love, I'm Mother.

Lawrence   Well, see if I'm gonna – excuse me – fuck 'em, I don't want words, words, words and games. I want – they gotta lie back and take it good.

Tull   And Kitty in't never gonna do that.

Lawrence   And Kitty in't never gonna do that. See, all I wants an honest simple – excuse me – fuck. I'm a pig-man. Thass low wages. And there's wife and eight infants to feed. And wife. Well, wife's insides got messed about with all that carrying and birthing, so wife, wife – excuse me – wife in't been worth fucking in years. So when I drive my pigs into market and selling's done, thass what I want. A – excuse me – fuck. Thass what makes life worth living. Do you understand?

Tull   Course, my love.

Lawrence   I dun't think woman can ever understand that.

Tull   Your woman muddles it all up, dun't she? Can't just lie back and – 'Take me.' It's all: 'Take me cos you love me.'

Lawrence   Thass right.

Tull   Or: 'Take me cos I want infant.'

Lawrence   Infants. Thass woman for you.

Tull   Well, I'm Mother Clap. And Clap – let's just say I've give up 'love me' and 'give me infant'.

Lawrence   And now what's left is . . .

Tull   What's left is . . .

Lawrence   What's left is 'fuck me'.

Tull   Well, I suppose that's right.

Pause.

Lawrence   Look, I in't really bothered about lads. The only reason I – excuse me – fuck lads is cos woman's needy and whores want paying. But you –

Tull   Yes?

Lawrence   Seems to me you're . . . woman who understands a fuck's a fuck. You're a – excuse me – fucking wonder.

Tull   You don't want me. Old thing. You want young –

Lawrence   I want a hole. I want to work away 'til my pleasure comes. And there'd be pleasure in that for you too seems to me.

Tull   I got work. Forty, forty-one, forty-two.

Lawrence   Come, can't be running about after sodomites all your life. Look to yourself. Look to me. Come to a private room. I spill easy. Wun't be more than a few minutes.

Tull   Oh, love. I'd like that. But . . .

Lawrence *kisses her.*

Lawrence   I dun't kiss as a rule.

Tull   Beer and tobacco. In't tasted that in a long time.

Lawrence   I want you – do something special. Make noise.

Tull   Wassat?

Lawrence   Make noise like –

Enter **Amy**.

Amy   They're calling out for more beer. Only there in't none.

Lawrence   You – leave us be.

Amy   Shall I fetch more beer?

Tull   Well, I suppose you better. Here.

Tull *gives* **Amy** *money.*

Amy   This one a bother?

Tull   You just run along.

Amy (*to* **Lawrence**)   I tell you, you're a bother, I'll run you through.

Tull   Thass enough, Ned. Off you run.

Exit **Amy**.

Lawrence   Whole world's gone arsey-versey. Now come, up to that room.

Tull   No. I in't doing that.

Lawrence   Well then – excuse me but – fuck you. I gotta get a hole. I got a lad willing if you in't gonna – give me the key.

Tull   You promise it in't Kitty Fisher?

Lawrence   Much better than that.

Tull   Then here. And may you find what you want.

Lawrence   Oh, how I wish it'd been you. Well – lad's just gonna have to take my anger now, inn'e?

*Lawrence kisses **Tull** and exits. **Tull** goes back to her money.*

Tull   Forty . . . oh, where was I? . . . forty . . . oh, come on, girl, where'd'you leave off? Forty, forty, forty. Forty what? One, two, three.

*Enter **Orme** followed by **Kedger** and **Philips**.*

Orme   Ma? You seen the pig-man?

Tull   Kitty love. Ma's counting.

Orme   The pig-man been in here?

Tull   Well, maybe he has and maybe he hasn't.

Orme   You didn't give him the key, did you, Ma?

Tull   I gotta concentrate.

Orme   Dun't tell me you give him the key.

Philips   Come, chuck, don't bother Ma now.

Orme   I gotta know: You give him the key?

Tull   Kitty – you gotta learn. Sun don't spin round you. Just cos you got fair face dun't mean you're the only one that's ever gonna be took. Dun't mean you're the only one pig-man's got his eye on.

Orme   Oh, I know that.

Tull   So maybe you learn from this you gotta be truer.

Orme   Has he got the key?

Tull   Yes. He's got the key. Eight, nine, ten.

Orme   Oh, fuck you, fuck you.

Orme *upsets the piles of money.*

Tull   Kitty!

Kedger   Come, love. Come to Ma and Pa.

Kedger *and* **Philips** *hold* **Orme**.

Orme   He's with Susan.

Tull   No.

Orme   Oh yes. 'See, it's me he wants not you,' says Susan. 'And he's gone to fetch the key.'

Tull   Oh Lord.

Orme   Can't bear to think of him taking my Susan.

Kedger   Your Susan?

Orme   My Susan.

Philips   But in't you always said . . .

Orme   Thass what I always said but now – new feeling. What's this I got inside me, Ma?

Tull   Close your eyes. What you see?

Orme   Green. Brightest green ever.

Tull   Then that's jealousy.

Orme   And is that a good feeling?

Tull   Thass lover's feeling.

Orme   Oh, I don't want to be a lover.

Tull   Then go back and dance and find another.

Philips   Come, chuck, away. Sisters waiting.

Orme, **Philips** *and* **Kedger** *go to exit.*

Orme   Oh, but I can't get Susan out my head. What's that pig-man doing to him, Ma?

Tull   Well, I don't know I'm sure. Old woman like me in't gonna know, is she? Come. Back to the dance.

Private room. **Martin** *and* **Lawrence**.

Martin   Locked now. All to ourselves.

Martin *slips the key into his cleavage.*

Lawrence   Lie down.

Martin   You're fast.

Lawrence   Man's always fast. That's his way.

Martin *lies on his back.*

Lawrence   Other way. On your front.

Lawrence *is getting out of his skirts — he still has his breeches on underneath.*

Martin   Oh, but in't we gonna buss a little?

Lawrence   No. Other way.

Martin   But there's always kisses here. See, if you're working down there, I like to feel you in here too.

Lawrence   And if I'm working down there, I don't want to feel nothing up here, see? So turn over.

Martin   One kiss. Just one kiss.

Lawrence   Come here.

They kiss.

Martin   You taste nice.

Lawrence   Thass the beer.

Martin *caresses* **Lawrence**'s *groin.*

Martin   Hello Peter, hello. That good?

Lawrence   S'alright.

Martin   Peter's still asleep, in't he? I'll have to wake him. Wake up, Peter. Wake up. No time to be a-bed. Oh yes. Cock is crowing. Toodleoodleooo! How much beer you had?

Lawrence   Fair amount.

Martin   Toooodleooo! Captain Pintle. Stand to attention. Bugle's going. Doodoodedoo! Oh yes, time to invade the lowlands. Forward march.

Lawrence   Here. Let me do it.

He works himself up.

Get on all fours.

Martin *is on the bed on his hands and knees.*

Martin   Do you like that? Is that how you want me?

Lawrence   Yeah. Like an animal. Like a big old sow. Titties hanging down and all them little pigs sucking on you. Make noise.

Martin   How you mean?

Lawrence   Make noise of a sow.

Martin   I in't never heard it.

Lawrence   Everyone's heard pigs.

Martin *attempts a pig noise.*

Lawrence   No. In't you ever been on a farm?

Martin   Never.

Lawrence   Like this. (*He makes a pig noise.*)

Martin *copies* **Lawrence**'s *noise.*

Lawrence   Thass good. Now. I'm a big old hog and I'm coming up to you.

Lawrence *makes aggressive hog noises.*

Martin   Come on then.

Lawrence   Since when has sows been talkers? Do as you're told.

With much grunting and squealing from both sides, **Lawrence** *enters* **Martin***.*

Martin   Thass – hurting.

Lawrence *grunts and squeals louder.*

Martin   Slower there. That hurts.

Lawrence   There's slaughterman, takes away hogs that are a bother, you know that? Well, he does. One of 'em goes wrong, hold 'em down and clean cut across the throat, see? So. You a good pig or a bad pig?

Martin   Good pig.

Lawrence   Right then.

He enters **Martin** *again. It is less painful for* **Martin** *this time.*

Lawrence   Oh yes. Oh yes. I'm nearly . . . yes.

Tull *and* **Orme** *appear outside the door.*

Tull   Susan? Susan love, you in there?

Lawrence   Ignore 'em.

Tull   Susan. Mother's got Kitty with her.

Martin   Then tell her: Susan's having a high old time. Oh yes! Yes! Yes!

Lawrence   No. Grunts only. Oh yes. I'm gonna spill, I'm gonna . . .

Tull   Susan, Kitty wants to speak to you.

Martin   I ain't speaking to Kitty. Take me, take me.

Lawrence   Thass it. Work me. I'm close.

Orme   Susan love −

Lawrence *grunts vigorously.*

Orme   Susan love. I been a wrong un. I see that now.
Susan? Them others? They was fucks and fucks is fucks but,
Susan, you − Susan, I love you. And love's love. And it's all
hurting and jealousy and wanting and it's bloody awful and
really I dun't want nothing to do with it − but I got it,
Susan. Susan −I got love for you.

Martin   Yeah?

Lawrence   Don't stop.

Orme   Thass true, Susan. Ev'ry blessed word.

Martin *pulls away from* **Lawrence**

Lawrence   Oh − fuck you.

Martin   You swear?

Orme   I swear. Open the door.

Lawrence   Come back. I'm so close.

Tull   Susan love −

Lawrence   You can't leave off now. Can't just work a
body up and leave him. Come, Mistress Sow.

Martin *turns the key in the lock.*

Lawrence   Oh no, no, no.

Tull *and* **Orme** *come into the room.*

Lawrence   Fuck it. Fuck it. Fuck it.

Orme   Oh, Susan love.

Martin   Oh, Kitty love.

Orme *and* **Martin** *kiss passionately.*

Lawrence   What about me? I'm only asking for a fuck. Is that too much to ask?

Martin   I didn't want to . . . just . . .

Orme   I know, love. Come away. Oh, Susan.

Exit **Martin** *and* **Orme**.

Lawrence   Look, I'm very close. I'm a breath away. Could you just . . . ?

Tull   No, love.

Lawrence   Oh well.

He turns away and masturbates until he comes.

Excuse me. Sorry. I hope I in't been a bother.

Tull   No, love, you in't.

Lawrence   Just when I get the ache . . . there's vulgarity and that and really with a woman around I shouldn't –

Tull   I understand. Here. Kiss for Ma.

She kisses him.

Lawrence   Oh well, back to the country. Back to my wife. Back to my pigs.

Exit **Lawrence**. **Tull** *is just about to go when: Enter* **Princess**. *He is in men's clothes.*

Princess   Howdeedo.

Tull   Oh, Princess.

Princess   No. In't Princess no more. Stopped all that now see. Gone back to me real name. William. How do I look to you?

Tull   Like a man.

Princess   Like any other man?

Tull   Yes. Like any other man.

Princess   Ordinary. Dull. Drab. Wouldn't you say?

Tull   Well, yes. Ordinary, dull, drab.

Princess   See, I thought couldn't keep hiding behind them skirts. Didn't want to do that no more. See, Mrs Tull. I think about you. All the time. Every minute. Church bell goes 'Tull', man calling out his wares cries 'Tull', open a door and it's creaking 'Tull'. And I can't just let that lie, can I?

Tull   Well, no. Suppose you can't.

Princess   So I had to come back to you and I wanted you to see me as I am. See William. And he in't special. But he cares about you.

Tull   Well, thass good. William.

Princess   Yes, Mrs Tull?

Tull   You wanna buss a little?

Princess   Yes, Mrs Tull.

They kiss.

Tull   See a man when you do that. Buss again.

Kiss again.

Tull   See a woman now.

Princess   No. Thass all finished now. I'm a man.

Tull   Saw a woman though.

Princess   Try again.

Kiss.

Tull   Yes. Definitely a woman.

Princess   Is that bad?

Tull   No. Felt good. Kiss me again.

Kiss.

Tull   Hermaphrodite.

Princess   Oh Lord. That wun't suppose to be.

Tull   Well, that's how it is. Man. Woman. Hermaphrodite.

Princess   Which of 'em do you want?

Tull   Well, now . . . Want a man . . .

Princess   Yes?

Tull   Want a woman . . .

Princess   Yes?

Tull   And I want . . . hermaphrodite. Want all of 'em. All of you. Oh, lustful thoughts.

Princess   Is that right?

Tull   Will you come to bed, love?

Princess   Mrs Tull . . . I'm a virgin.

Tull   And I in't much in practice but . . . You frightened?

Princess   A little.

Tull   I'll be gentle, love. Now come – to bed. Howdeedo, Princess.

Princess   Howdeedo.

Scene Ten

2001. **Tina** *sits on the sofa. Enter* **Edward**.

Edward   How you doing?

Tina   Yeah. Alright.

Edward   Thought we were going to lose you.

Tina   No. That's just him.

Edward   Bit of a drama queen?

Tina   No. He makes a fuss. I'm alright.

Enter **Charlie**.

Charlie   You sure you don't want an ambulance take you up the hospital?

Tina   No.

Charlie   If you want I can call –

Tina   No.

Charlie   I called your mum.

Tina   You didn't?

Charlie   You want a taxi take you home?

Tina   I dunno.

Charlie   I'll call a taxi. (*Dials mobile.*) Yeah, hello. Can I have a cab to –

Exit **Charlie**.

Tina   See what I mean? Says to me: Have anything you want, go anywhere you want. He's always buying me things and taking me places. Fly me right round the world if that's what I want. I can't stand it.

Edward   Sounds alright to me.

Tina   It's always you choose, babe, you decide. But I can't choose. I just wanna pierce myself. To pass the time. And it doesn't mean anything. Nothing means anything, does it?

Edward   No. Probably not.

Enter **Tom**.

Tom   Basically, I'm a very positive person. So I'm not going to let this get me down. I'm going to learn from this. Because this was a real experience. And that can't be bad, can it? It's like E, isn't it? Like good E and bad E. And if you never took like a really shit E – like E that is basically just a bit of speed and a load of shit – then you wouldn't like really appreciate a totally fantastic E that gets you off your tits until you look at the world and go 'I love you. I love you, world. You're fucking fantastic, you are.' Which is actually what happens more often than not with E. See, I reckon in a few years' time I'm going to be – no offence – really old. And then there'll be time to be sad and serious and all that – but until then it's like Global Disco Family. Am I talking shit?

Tina   Yes.

Tom   Sorry. Does anyone know a club that's still open?

Enter **Will**.

Tom   Excuse me. Do you know a club that's still open?

Will   No. Sorry. (*To* **Tina**.) Well, you're looking much better. (*To* **Edward**.) Thank Christ somebody knew what to do, eh?

Edward   Mmmmm.

Tina   What did you . . . ?

Will (*indicates* **Edward**)   Gave you the kiss of life.

Tina   What? You . . . ?

Edward   Yes. Old trick I picked up somewhere.

Tina   Right. Right.

Enter **Charlie**.

Charlie   Taxi's on its way, babe.

Enter **Josh** *and* **Phil**.

Josh (*to* **Will**)   Listen, we thought we'd go on to a club. You want to come?

Will   No. I'll clean up the mess. I'll see you tomorrow.

Phil (*to* **Edward**)   You coming?

Edward   I don't think so. Rather a lot of editing to do. Not one of our better efforts but still . . . should be able to salvage something. Yes. Video and a bit of a tug on the old love stick and then bed for me, I reckon. (*To* **Josh**.) He's a fantastic fuck. You'll have a great time.

Tom   Take me with you. I won't be a bother. Just I need to share the taxi only I haven't got enough . . .

Josh   Sure. Why not? See you tomorrow.

Exit **Josh**, **Phil** *and* **Tom**.

Charlie   Sorry about the mess.

Will   These things happen.

Charlie   And when you want some gear . . .

Will   Of course. Always going to need a bit of gear, aren't we? Got to be something, make this bearable.

Charlie   Yeah. Right. Right. Well, then, see ya.

A car horn sounds.

Charlie (*to* **Tina**)   Taxi's here. You alright to walk or do you want me to . . . ?

Tina   Fuck off.

Charlie   Yeah. Right. Right. Fucking headcase.

Exit **Tina** *and* **Charlie**.

Edward   D'you see what happened to the butt plug? Got lost somewhere in the mêlée.

Edward *starts searching.*

Will   Don't you ever . . . ?

Edward   Yes?

Will   Don't you want to say: You're mine. And I want you to myself and I can't stand this fucking around. It's killing me.

Edward   Oh no. No fun in that at all, is there?

Will   No, suppose not. Oh fuck. Look at this sofa.

Edward   Soon get that off. Good scrub's all it needs. Now where's my . . . ? Bathroom?

Exit **Edward**.

Will   Oh, fuck it. Fuck it. Fuck it.

Scene Eleven

'Motto 6'

God
> The pain of love is hard to bear
> The joy of love is strong
> And lovers come and fuck and leave
> But business carries on
> Oh business carries on
> Enterprise shall light your darkness
> Business must go on.

The molly house. A large trunk with its lid open. **Tull** *is packing the trunk with linen, pewter, etc. She sings to herself as she goes.*

Enter **Princess**. *He is wearing his dress. He is carrying a heavily laden bag.*

Tull   Oh yes. Dun't you look fine? Wass it like – back in the rig?

Princess   Feels good. I thought . . . somedays skirts, somedays breeches. What do you think?

Tull   Oh yes. Variety's the spice, innit? Let's say breeches or dress during the week and then Sundays . . . (*Laughs.*)

Princess (*laughs*)   Yes?

Tull   Well, on Sundays, Lord's day . . .

Princess   Yes?

Tull   Hows about we Adam and Eve it on Sundays?

Princess   What . . . ?

Tull   Naked as we were born all the day long.

Princess   Oh yes. Naked as we were born. But what if there should be passers-by?

Tull   Then fuck 'em – for in't that how the Lord made us?

Princess   Still – dun't wanna upset neighbours.

Tull   Then you must rig us up lovely out of leaves. Be leaves a-plenty in the country, I should think. Oooo – Sunday can't come fast enough, says I.

They carry on packing.

Princess   You wanna take the ledger?

Tull   No. Ledger's all part of the effects. She's gonna need ledger, in't she? not me.

Princess   Still, we gotta live . . .

Tull   You telling me how to do business?

Princess   No, love.

Tull   I can do business. Don't you fret yourself on that score. I'm renting the house and the business for a good price, see? Just cos I got love in my heart now dun't mean me head can't do numbers, dun't mean these hands can't count coin. So I drove her hard and now we can stretch to a bit of land. And I shall turn my hand to husbandry and you can take in sewing. How does that do you?

Princess   That does me as fine as Heaven on Earth.

Tull   Well and it don't come better than that.

*Enter **Martin**. He is in men's clothes and he is carrying luggage and the 'baby'.*

Martin   Are you petting?

Tull   No, love, we're working.

Martin   Only I'll leave you be if you're . . .

Tull   No, love. Come on. Soon be time to go.

Princess   You tired, boy?

Tull   That was his Kitty Fisher keeping him up.

Martin   No. That was . . . that was . . .

Tull   Was we being awful noisy?

Martin   Terrible noisy.

Tull   Making up for wasted years, in't we, Princess? The old uns is the worst uns, dun't you think?

Martin   I should say.

Pause. He holds up the 'baby'.

I was wandering. Found . . . What d'you wanna do with this? I was gonna leave it. But then I thought . . . maybe Ma wants to play that game. Of an evening, I can, or Kitty can, or you can . . . take it in turns to give birth if that's what Ma wants. What do you say?

Tull   I say . . . I say . . . trunks is awful full and I say . . . best leave the infant behind. Thass what I say.

Martin   You sure?

Tull   Yes, love, I'm sure. In't time for them games no more, is it? Old woman Tull – that's her wanting, that is. And I dun't want none of that foolish bitch no more. And Mother Clap. She's gone too. Goodbye to her. Dun't need me mollies a-skipping and a-fucking around me no more. Good game while it lasted and it filled me purse fit to bursting. So now we can move on. Away from this world. And on to the new. Whatever we are. Just the four of us. Princess, Kitty, Susan and . . . Lord, who am I?

Princess   Wassat?

Tull   If I in't Tull and I in't Clap, who am I?

Martin   Mother?

Tull   No. Not Mother. New name for me. But what? Well, time will tell.

Enter **Orme** *and* **Amelia**. **Orme** *carries several dresses.*

Amelia   Oh no, boy. Just you leave them be.

Orme   But that's my dress. / I wanna take my dress.

Amelia   Oh no. Not yours to take, see? They're mine.

Orme   Ma, you tell her – that's my dress and she in't having it.

Tull   Well, Kitty love, that in't strictly –

Orme   Oh, ma, can't live without me dress.

Tull   Well, see, I've leased it all. Lock, stock and gown. It's all hers now.

Amelia   And I hire out at a shilling a day. So . . . Of course if you wanna stay in London and hire 'em then I might consider . . .

Tull   Thought you was gonna tally to whores.

Amelia   Well, now, Mrs Tull, I've been giving that some thought.

Tull   Thass what you told me.

Amelia   I know that's what I said. But then . . . well, then the Lord spoke to me.

Tull   Oh, did he now?

Amelia   Oh yes, Lord spoke. And he said to me: It's a bugger's world. And he said: Your man don't really like your woman. And he said: All your man wants to do is find a hole and work away and he said: Arse will always triumph over cunt.

Tull   Oh no, I don't think that's right.

Amelia   And I was sore afraid. And for three days and three nights I fretted. Because what's it gonna be like? In this bugger's world. Bugger King, bugger merchant, bugger cowman. And every maid lost and alone. And not a child born. And soon world'll be empty, just animals like man had never been.

Tull   No. That in't never gonna happen.

Amelia   But still the Lord called me and I thought molly house is full and whore house is empty and so I decided: don't tally, molly. It's the only way to survive. And that's what I intend to do.

Enter **Cranton** *and* **Bolton**.

Amelia   And these girls will run and fetch for me. Isn't that so, girls?

Cranton/Bolton   Yes, Mother.

Tull   Well, just you be good to them mollies, mind.

Amelia   Course, Mrs Tull. Customers are always treated kindly, aren't they, girls?

Cranton/Bolton   Yes, Mother.

Tull   Oh, I hope so.

Amelia (*to* **Orme**)   So come, boy. Tonight's gonna be a grand old night at Mother's. Take who you will. Will you hire and stay?

Orme   Is it gonna be as good as Clap's?

Amelia   It's gonna be better than Clap's.

Orme   Well, that sounds awful good.

Martin   But, love – what about country? What about cottage?

Orme   Oh, Susan. I dun't know whether I can live out all me days in a cottage. Thass her dream. Thass running away from the world. And I in't ready to do that.

Amelia   Then hire, boy, and fuck away.

Orme   Susan – maybe if I stayed tonight. Just for old times. And then I could come to you tomorrow.

Martin   If that's what you want.

Orme   That's what I want.

Amelia   That's it, boy.

Orme   And maybe from time to time I can come a-mollying and maybe if you wanna come a-mollying too . . .

Martin   Well, we'll have to see about that.

Orme   Yes. We'll have to see about that.

Enter **Kedger**, **Philips** *and several* **Mollies** *– all in men's clothes.*

Kedger   Coach is waiting, Ma. Come to make our goodbyes.

Tull   Goodbye, my chucks. Goodbye.

Goodbyes are made. The **Mollies** *help carry out the trunks and luggage as this is done.*

Tull   Well, in't we had some high old times but Ma's gotta go now.

Enter **Amy**, *still dressed as Ned.*

Bolton   Amy. What you done to yourself, girl?

Amy (*to* **Tull**)   Country in't the place you think it is. Country's hard. Thieving and raping in the country same as here. You're gonna need a man looking over you in the country.

Tull   You wanna come with us, Ned?

Amy   You're gonna need me.

Tull   Then you come with us, Ned. There's a place for you.

Philips   Coach won't wait no more.

Tull   Come, loves, away.

Exit **Tull**, **Princess** *and* **Amy**. **Martin** *rushes up to* **Orme**.

Martin   You'll come tomorrow?

Orme   Susan, you musn't nag.

Martin   I'll be waiting for you.

Orme   Well, that's good.

Tull (*off*)   Susan! Susan!

Martin *exits.* **Mollies** *gather round the door and wave them off. The coach's horn sounds until it becomes distant and fades. The* **Mollies** *turn back to* **Amelia**.

Amelia   Well and off she goes. But you musn't feel low. Because we're carrying on. And I'm Mother now. And Mother's purse is hungry. So – come. Fill.

The **Mollies** *don't move.*

Orme   Come, sisters.

Amelia   They in't coming, boy.

Orme   What, sisters, off away? And where are you to go? Back into the dark? Oh no. Can't do that.
    So come. Here we can jig and drink and fuck. And anyone of you as wants Kitty Fisher can have me.
    Sisters. This is the best we got.
    So: pay!

The **Mollies** *fill* **Amelia**'s *purse.*

Amelia   That's it. And now dance, you buggers, dance.

Orme   Music!

'Amelia's 'Maggot'

The **Mollies** *start to dance.*

Amelia   That's it. Beer there beer.

Cranton *and* **Bolton** *fetch beer. The dancing becomes livelier.*

Orme   Oh yes. Dance. Dance. Dance. And on for ever more.

The dancing becomes more and more frenzied. **Eros** *joins the dancers. The* **Mollies** *start to take their clothes off. The music turns into techno. The molly house becomes a rave club as the light fades to nothing.*

Music

In the Royal National Theatre production of *Mother Clap's Molly House*, the accompaniment for 'End of Act One' and 'Pleasure' was pre-recorded. The remainder of the music was played by a five-piece pit band with orchestrations by Matthew Scott. The full score and band parts, and both pre-recorded accompaniments, are available on hire from the play's agent, Casarotto Ramsay & Associates Ltd, Waverley House, 7–12 Noel Street, London W1F 8GQ.

These songs were written to be performed by actors who sang, rather than specifically for singers, and hence there are fewer strict allocations of vocal parts than is traditional. The majority of the songs were performed by male voices (with obvious exceptions) but productions should feel free to adjust where necessary to accommodate whatever balance of genders they prefer.

Further information on the music can be found on the composer's website: www.matthewscott.net or via the play's agent.

Words: Mark Ravenhill

Opening Act One

Music: Matthew Scott

114

Opening Act One

En - ter-prise come light our dark - ness Bus' - ness shape our heart and hand

Then oh rich our Fath-er migh- ty Lead us to the Prom - ised land

Words: Mark Ravenhill

Music: Matthew Scott

Funeral, Motto 2 and Wake

The wid - ow's in a sor - ry state with hus - band dead and

Funeral Motto 2 and Wake

crumble on cue

Music: Matthew Scott

Wake 2

Music: Matthew Scott

Wake 3

Motto 3 and Eros' Song 1

Words: Mark Ravenhill

Music: Matthew Scott

Motto Three

Motto Three

My ar - row's sharp, my bow is stretched, Here's E - ros here's de - light.

here's de - light. A - rise,____ a - rise,____ Up up and

rise and ri - sen fol - low me._____ And ri - sen fol low_

122

Motto Three

Motto Three

Motto Three

me. And com - ing think of____ com - ing think of____ And

com - ing think of me.

Motto 4: New Stock

Words: Mark Ravenhill

Music: Matthew Scott

128

Words: Mark Ravenhill

Music: Matthew Scott

Motto Five: Dame Fortune

End of Act One

Words: Mark Ravenhill

Music: Matthew Scott

Rejoice - End of Act One

132

Rejoice - End of Act One

134

Rejoice - End of Act One

call this sod-o-my___ We call it fab - u-lous

Fab - u-lous

fab - u lous   Shit on those who call this sod-o-my it's

Fa - a - bu-lous

END OF ACT ONE

PHOEBUS Reprise

Words: Mark Ravenhill

Music: Matthew Scott

136

Phoebus Reprise

Er - os still the hand of Time___ May Youth be ev - er___ yours___

Saxes ∞

C   G/B   E7 Am   Esus

___ With Age comes grief but youth is free so play___ and

E   C/E   F♯sus   Am/C   Bsus   CΔ

Enter MOLLIES   (BLIND MANS BLUFF)

leave re - morse

[+Cym]

Bsus   Em

Phoebus Reprise

Words: Mark Ravenhill

Music: Matthew Scott

Mother Claps Maggot
(Jig pre-Fine Fucking)

Words: Mark Ravenhill

Music: Matthew Scott

Fine Fucking

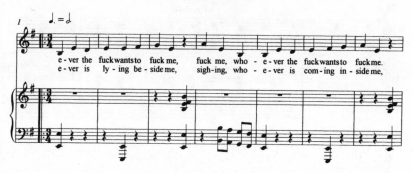

e - ver the fuck wants to fuck me, fuck me, who - e - ver the fuck wants to fuck me.
e - ver is ly - ing be - side me, sigh - ing, who - e - ver is com - ing in - side me,

Fuck me 'cos you are the fi - nest, the fi - nest I've fucked, the fi - nest, the
dy - ing, the stran - ger, the stran - ger I'm fuck - ing the bet - ter, but clo - sing my

allargando - - - - - -

1.
fi - nest, the fi - nest I've fucked. Who -
eyes,____ I

2.
still see your face, so we'll

140

Birthing Scene

Music: Matthew Scott

Segue "Pleasure"

142

Pleasure

Words: Mark Ravenhill

Music: Matthew Scott

144

146

REPEAT AND FA

The Whore's Prayer

Words: Mark Ravenhill

Music: Matthew Scott

148

The Whore's Prayer

150

Words: Mark Ravenhill

Music: Matthew Scott

Motto Six

GOD:

The pain of love is hard to bear

Clarinets

The joy of love is strong   And   lov - ers come and   fuck and leave   but

bus' ness carr - ies   on,   Oh bus' ness   carr - ies   on

151

Motto Six 29-8-01

En - ter - prise shall light your dark - ness Bus' ness must go

on

Music: Matthew Scott

Amelia's Maggot

Segue Club Mus

Product

Product was first presented by Mark Ravenhill and Paines Plough at the Traverse Theatre, Edinburgh, on 17 August 2005. The cast was as follows:

James	Mark Ravenhill
Olivia	Elizabeth Baker
Director	Lucy Morrison
Lighting and Sound Designer	Mat Ort

An office. **James**, *a film producer and* **Olivia**, *an actress.*

James So there's a knife.

And your eyes widen as you see the knife.

And he's pulled it out from under his . . . the knife comes out from . . . he's wearing a, a . . . robe.

He's a tall fellow, a tall, dusky fellow, and –

And now he uses the knife, he uses the knife and he slits open the plastic on his croissant and he puts the croissant in his mouth and he puts the knife in that sort of stringy pouch in front of him.

Now you want to call out – you are just about to call out:

'He's got a knife. The tall dusky fellow has got a knife.'

But something – a decision, a small but important beat, you don't call out. You look down the aisle at the tanned and blond and frankly effeminate airline staff and you don't call out.

Why? Why? Why? Well . . .

Let's just discover her, shall we? Let's just discover Amy, a beat at a time.

'Excuse me,' you tells the dusky fellow, 'that's my seat.' You've had the window seat since childhood and he stands to let you in and you open the overhead baggage container – your luggage is Gucci, Gucci are in, it's going to be fabulous, you open the luggage container and . . .

There's a mat. A small oriental mat rolled up very neat.

Hold on your face. Suprise, apprehension, maybe, I just want you to . . . play it.

'Is this yours?'

'Yes.'

'Do you do yoga?'

'No. That is my prayer mat. I pray.'

'Oh.'

And you sit and you . . . you look out the window and
you . . . fear . . . you're in an, an aeroplane up in the air,
next to a tall dusky fellow whose prayer mat is up above
you and whose knife is in the pouch in front of you.

'Ladies and gentlemen. Could I remind you to switch off all
electrical goods?'

And you reach into your bag and you take out your mobile
and you go to switch off your mobile phone and now
we – close up on you – you look down at the mobile and
something is triggered inside you, a chord of emotion
resonates and we see – ah! Amy is wounded, there's a
wound and it's something about the mobile, something
about the . . . it's a narrative hook and it's empathy.

I know you're going to love her. I hope you're going to love
her. She is three-dimensional. And I'd love to see you play
three-dimensional again after those last three, four . . .

And now the fellow turns, he turns, the tall dusky, fellow he
turns and suddenly his head is on the shoulder of your suit –
it's Versace, Versace are on board, it's a Versace suit – his
dusky head is on the fabulous shoulder of your fabulous
Versace suit and he falls asleep.

And you look at, you look at him . . . You . . . His smell is so
different.

And do you know what you want to do? Do you know what
you want to do? Well, I'll . . .

You want to . . . you actually want to . . . you want to reach
out to the knife . . . reach out to the knife and you want to
grab hold of the knife, okay, and pull the knife out of that
stringy pouch and you want to feel the weight of the blade
in your hand and then you want to thrust it into him, in and
out and in and and in and out and in out until there is
blood, there is blood shooting from that dusky frame and

the blood is shooting over you and you're more blood than face and you want to call out:

'This is for the Towers. This is for civilisation. This is for all of us, you bastard.'

You don't say that. You don't do that. That's an interior monologue. You play that? I want you to play that with your eyes. Can you play that with your . . . ? Well of course you can, of course you can. I love your work.

'This is for all of us you bastard.'

You see? You see? Amy is wounded. She is . . . to each of us the wound, to each the wound is different. It sounds classical but it's me, it's my note to my writers . . . show me the wound . . . and . . . please . . . I will show you Amy's wound if you'll – Yes? Yes? Yes?

It's a thrill to have you in the room.

So Amy doesn't touch the knife, she leaves the knife, the knife is untouched and the plane lands and the dusky fellow puts the knife under his robe and he takes his prayer mat from the baggage container and that should be . . . they should never meet again but . . . this is the world of the heart, this is the screen, the dream, this is movie-land, so, so, so . . .

It's a rainy night, a storm at Heathrow, a broken heel on your Jimmy Choos and the only taxi left and it's his taxi, and suddenly he's saying:

'Please – get in.'

Fear but somehow excitement. The adventure has begun. Into the car of a stranger.

And you climb in with fear and excitement and there's the prayer mat and there's the knife on the seat between him and you, and you:

'Which way are you going?'

'I don't know. Which way you going?'

'I – I – I – '

'You gonna take me home?'

Take him home? Take him home? Are you going to take
him home?

Cut to your face. Cut to the knife. Cut to the prayer mat.
Cut to his – and the lighting favours him now, okay?
Something in the lighting – for the first time he looks
handsome.

And you, and you, and you – you play the, her aching
sexuality. Which I know you . . .

Your sexuality aches and he's handsome and you ignore the
prayer mat and the knife and you say to the cabbie,

'The docklands please.'

And he says,

'Docklands love, course love.'

And you exit east from Trafalgar Square.

You live in an abbatoir, it's an old converted abbatoir that is
now a massively cool loft-style apartment and it feels good
to be home and strange and exciting to be letting the dusky
fellow in to your world, but you open the door and you let
him in and he puts down the knife and the prayer mat on
your floor and you offer him wine, but he doesn't drink, but
you do drink –

And you're nervous and you drink the better part of a bottle
and your eye occasionally flicks to the knife and the prayer
mat and now you've drunk the bottle and you are . . .

'I'm Amy. I open call centres and call centres, I travel
around and around and around in dwindling circles around
this shrinking globe.'

A man, a tall, dusky man in your apartment.

Your sexuality is so . . . it's aching, it's aching . . . it's
inflamed and you – you suprise yourself – but you want

him, you want him, you want the dusky fellow and you, and
you press yourself upon him.

Mohammed.

But he's frightened. He's a virgin and he knows nothing of
this world of aching sexuality and he's frightened.

'Amy, I'm frightened.'

'Mohammed, don't be frightened. Don't be . . . Ssssh. Ssssh.
Ssssh.'

And you lead him to the bed and it's very beautiful – and
you have a body double, Beata is your body double – and
you lead him to the bed and you slip his body from his robes
and at last your ache can be, can be, can be . . . filled.

And he is slow and unsure and clumsy at first, but then as
you move together, body and heart and . . . as you find the
music of your . . . and now you begin to come and come
and come and come and come and it's the orgasm of your
life.

To find yourself, to find yourself, you – Amy – with your
wound, to find yourself so at one with this dusky fellow is so
. . . strange. We have to . . . we have to see that in your face.
Can you play that? Can you . . . ? Of course. I love your
work. I love it. I've seen you do those turns on a sixpence.
Hate. Love. Click. Power. Subjection. Click. I've seen you
do that with a shit script and a cast I wouldn't wish on a
mini-series. You're fabulous and this is fab – it's gonna be
fabulous once it's been punched up.

But then – time passes in the night – time passes in the night
and maybe you fall asleep but you wake, you wake – a jolt –
uh – and you reach out – you reach out – you reach out and
– you're – like so many times before you're alone in the bed.

Has he – ? Has he gone? Has he taken you and gone?

Your eyes adjust to the darkness. No. He hasn't gone. He
hasn't . . . There is the prayer mat and there is the knife just

where he left them on your floor, so he hasn't gone he's just, he's . . .

And then you see him. You see his dusky frame. You see the dusky frame moving about your incredibly cool loft-style apartment – which was once an abbatoir – and you see him and he's moving about and he's looking at your white goods and he's looking at your black goods and your chrome goods and your beech goods and your plasma and your bluetooth and your exercise equipment and you know, you know, you know what he's doing and you throw yourself, you throw your naked – Beata's naked body from the bed and the words just come up, they just come up from inside you and you scream:

'Stop judging me. Stop fucking judging. So my life is worthless. So I'm busy but it means nothing. So all I have around me is clutter and no value. So I never had a belief. So I'm all alone and I'll let the first human being inside me who shows me the slightest – '

'So, so, so, so – '

(We had a theatre writer work on this bit.)

'And you, what about you? Who gives you your orders? The Imam? The Dictator? Allah? Oh, open your eyes, open your eyes. What would you like to do to me eh? Given half a chance. Cover me up? Stone me? But you'd like to.'

That's stopped him. That's stopped him in his tracks and he's just stopped and he's listening to you.

'How can you, how dare you feel superior to me? I am freedom, I am progress, I am democracy – and you are fear and darkness and evil and I hate you.'

His sperm is still dribbling down your leg. That's a private note. We won't shoot it.

And now you, there are tears, you are, the tears come up and now – your wound – as if on impulse, a beat, fast beat, you reach for your mobile and you call up a message, a message from the past, a message from – the time when the wound began, when all the hurting began to hurt.

And you – message is on conference and you place it there in the middle of the floor down by the prayer mat and down by the knife, and you place your mobile phone down and you stand naked and Mohammed stands naked – like Eve, like Eve – and you listen to:

'Oh my God oh my God oh my God oh my God oh my God . . . ' (It can be punched up.)

'Oh my God Amy, something's got the tower. They've . . . the other tower is on fire.'

'And – Amy, sweetheart, I think they've got us too. I think they hit our tower, sweetheart. We're on fire. Shit. We're on fire. And I'm gonna have to jump baby and I – I just want you to know, Amy, I love you, I love you, I love you with all my – aaaaah.'

And the message ends and Amy falls, falls to the floor and sobs. Which I think you can, I know you can . . .

I get a lot of scripts. It's my job. I get . . . there are hundreds of thousands of stories and they're sitting on my desk and mostly they are, they are, they are . . .

The effluent of the soul.

Nobody understands the basic, the truth, the wound.

But this script, this story, I – I have been touched, I have been moved by this. When I – I have lain on the floor in my office and wept when I read this script, you see? You see?

And I want to . . .

There are powers greater than me. There is a Higher Power. I cannot greenlight. And I have been to the Power and I have said: 'This is the one, this is the . . . I want to produce this script, I have wept like a woman at this script and now I must tell this story,' and the Power has said to me: 'Get someone big attached.'

And so I – so I – so I – no bullshit – I thought of you. For
Amy. You are my first, you are my only choice for Amy –

Because like her you are . . . I know you hurt, I know . . . it's
there, it's up there on the screen, your raw wound for me, us
all to see which is why you . . .

You fascinate and you excite me.

So let's . . . make a movie.

The message ends. The message from the past, the message
from the Towers, and Amy falls to the floor of her fabulous
apartment and she is sobbing and now she, she's calling out:

'Troy's gone. I'll never see Troy again. Troy died in the
Towers and I'll never see Troy again.'

And Mohammed comes to you and he puts his arms around
you.

'Ssssshhh.'

And for a moment, there's comfort, comfort, but then your
POV on the knife and the prayer mat and you say:

'Mohammed, I have to know. I have to know, Mohammed.'

'Sssshhh. Not now Amy.'

'Yes, Mohammed I have to – are you Al Queda?'

'Not now, Amy. Ssssh. Sssssssh. Sssssh.'

And he lies you down on the bed and he holds you and, oh,
the comfort of that dusky frame.

Now let's not play Amy with any judgement please, no let's
not judge . . . let's just . . . let's just play her as a woman, as
a woman who that night as she lay there fell in love, fell in
love with a man, a man with a knife and a prayer mat, a
woman who that night as she slept, as she slept in
Mohammed's dusky arms, forgot, forgot for the first time
since the eleventh of the ninth of 2001, forgot the smoke
and the confusion and the calls, and the droop and crumble
of the Towers, and she forgot the fall of Troy.

And let's – moment by moment, day by day – she is drawn
into Mohammed's world, moment by moment, day by day,
and other men begin to gather at her apartment, other men
with their robes and their knives and their prayer mats –
seven, then eight, then nine, then ten men at a time, their
mats positioned on the floor, calling to Mecca, talking,
planning.

Is this is a cell? Is this – a fundamentalist terrorist threat in
the middle of your world?

You should ask, you should challenge, but you're – it's love,
you're in – wild, blind, stupid – and the Heart is a bigger
organ than the Brain, as we say in this business we call
show.

And then one day they are there – Mohammed and the
men are there with their knives and their prayer mats in
your fabulous loft-style apartment, and you're making their
infusion and suddenly the door opens, the door opens
and you turn and you see, you see, you see, here, in your
apartment, coming across your apartment, he's there in your
apartment, in your apartment, Osama is in your apartment.

And he comes towards you and he smiles at you – it's a
cruel smile – and he . . .

Bless you.

Why don't you – ? There are knives, there are – Why don't
you attack? You could, you should, you –

It's inner conflict you're experiencing, you're playing this
inner conflict. Everything is – for the sake of Troy, for
revenge you should attack, you should revenge but you
don't and you are kissed – you are kissed, a warm breathy
kiss on the forehead from Osama.

And now the plan is revealed. Now the work of the cell is
made known to you. Now you know that they are all evil
men.

Europe is to be torn apart. The Hague. The Reichstag.
Tate Modern. Suicide bombing. Each of these men is to be
stuffed and strapped with explosives and then at midday
tomorrow they will carry off buildings and people and
nothing but misery and devastation will follow.

And now they're coming to Mohammed. To Mohammed's
task. What will be Mohammed's task?

You want to cry out:

'No, no, no, no, Mohammed. I love you.'

Your mouth is open but the words don't come.

And then you discover, then you learn. Osama turns, he
turns and he gives Mohammed his mission: Disneyworld
Europe. He must blow up Disneyworld Europe.

And now you step forward and you hear yourself saying, as
if another is speaking for you:

'I can't bear for you to do this, Mohammed. I can't bear to
lose you. I've already lost Troy. And I won't lose you. I'm a
woman and I love this man.'

And then you turn to Osama.

'Let me go with him. Strap me and stuff me with explosives
and let me go with him and let me die with my man in the
middle of the day, in the middle of the continent, at
Disneyworld Europe.'

'No woman can ever – '

'Please, great mullah, please. I am a woman but I love this
man and I want to die with this man.'

Minutes go by and we cut to the faces of the jihadists as they
wait for the decision of Osama, their mullah. Cut to
Mohammed – his eyes are misty. Cut to you – waiting,
waiting.

And then Osama breathes and he smiles and he nods:

'Yes.'

You are to die with your man.

And that night you lie in Mohammed's arms, you lie and wait the call that will take you to the EuroStar and on to your mission, you lie in the dark and he says:

'I love you, Amy, I love you with all my heart and I thank Allah for your bravery to join me in suicide.'

'It's just something I have to do, Mohammed.'

'But I fear. When my body is blown apart at the beat of twelve I will go to Paradise. It will be easy to leave this world and go to Paradise. Where will you go?'

'I . . . I . . . I . . . I . . . don't know Mohammed. Where there . . . Can I come to Paradise?'

'No. You are not chosen for Paradise.'

'Oh.'

'These are our last hours together.'

'Then fuck me. Fuck me. Fuck me. Fuck me these last few hours. Fill me every way you can until I hurt and I just can't take you any more. Come, Mohammed, come.'

'A place that only we know.'

And he does and you are hungry, hungry, hungry, but finally you're en-seam-ed bodies topple into slumber and then it comes, the nightmare comes.

You are there, you are in Disneyworld Europe and you are stuffed and strapped with every explosive known to man and you look around – a minute to twelve and you look around – and you see the people and you can't see . . . These are good people, these are good, fat, happy, bright people. Queueing, eating, riding people. These are your people. What are you doing? What are you doing?

Forty seconds until you take them away. Forty seconds until you push your hand through all of us and rip it apart.

How can you do this? Why are you doing this?

'Avez-vous vu ma mère?'

You look down at the little girl with the ears and the balloon and she's what – three?

'Avez-vous vu ma mère? Je veux ma mère. S'il vous plaît – je cherche ma mère.'

And you want to scream:

'No fucking point sweetheart. No fucking point. She's a dead person. I'm a dead person. You're a dead person. We're all just dead people in the Magic Kingdom of Life.'

But you don't – you take her hand – twenty seconds to go, but you take her hand –

You, you suicide jihadist, you take the hand of the pretty little girl with her mouse ears and balloon and you begin to walk down main street because you think: better she has these last few seconds of comfort in the search for *maman* than to die alone and in fear and despair.

The time is coming in now, it's coming – ten, nine, eight, seven, six –

The explosives on your body are pulsating and vibrating as if to will themselves to their deathly task –

Five –

'Mama, mama, où est-tu, mama?'

Four –

A figure is approaching.

'Bonjour – Je m'appelle Mickey. Vous est ma amie. Comment t'appelles-tu?'

'I am Death. I am Death. Run, Mickey. Run, Magic Kingdom. I am Death.'

Three –

'Bonjour – fille jolie. Quelle ballon joli.'

'*Où est mama?*'

Two –

'*Je ne sais pas. Moi, je ne suis pas ta mère.*'

One. Tiny beat – maybe it's not gonna, maybe it's not – maybe fate and computer error have saved the world but then –

Boom!

From your back and your chest and your sex the force comes, the explosive comes, and in your last moment of your life that child's head, now ripped from its body, and the blood filling your eyes, that child's head is blown towards you and her voice fills your head as you die:

'*Maman.*'

You wake with a start. It's three in the morning, three in the morning in your fabulous loft-style apartment and you look at Mohammed and suddenly you are filled with disgust.

What is this? What are you doing?

He shouldn't be here with you. He shouldn't be – he should be in an orange jump suit and he should be spat at and kicked and humiliated.

You pig. You dog. You worse than animal. Roll in this shit. Piss your pants. Eat your faeces, cunt.

And you are resolved and you reach for the phone and you phone the Special Forces.

And you report everything – sometimes with tears, sometimes in anger – you tell the whole terrible tale.

And now a van is on its way to take . . . Mohammed and the explosives.

Alone again. Another man who turned out to be not right for you. Every year the hurt grows a little more, until one day it will be so raw you'll never love.

Just one last look, one last look at Mohammed before he goes.

He looks like a boy – who could have thought he would be . . . ? He looks like a boy.

And you move towards him and you sit on the bed and you run your fingers through his dark, dark hair.

'I'm sorry, Mohammed, I'm sorry.'

And you lean forward and you kiss a gentle kiss upon the sleeping lips.

'Bitch.'

His eyes snap open, his hand is up and strikes across the jaw.

'Bitch. Bitch. Bitch.'

'Ahhh!'

'Bitch. You have betrayed us.'

His lithe body jumps from the bed and he kicks you in the stomach, there's no breath in your lungs, there's a gob of blood in your mouth.

'You have betrayed Allah.'

'I won't do it. I won't kill innocent children.'

And you fear for your life. You fear that Mohammed will kill you, dismembered corpse in your apartment, and you remember Mohammed's knife. And something inside you says – get the knife – get the knife – it's lying there and he could use the fucking knife and slit me toe to crown. You rush for the knife, you hold it – and you look up. But he hasn't gone for the knife.

He's got a petrol can in his hand. Where did that come from?

He looks down at you. His eyes lock on to yours. The seconds pass. A lorry passes in the night carrying beef to Dover. (That's a detail.)

And now there is sadness in his eyes and he says:

'I am the weakness. I am the flaw. I was the lust that drove me to woman. I have betrayed jihad.'

And he pours the petrol can over his dusky frame, shaking his hair like a girl in a shower after hockey.

'This world is a place of suffering and unhappiness. Yes?'

'Yes, yes, yes.'

'Please, Allah, admit me to Paradise, please Allah. I failed jihad, but please, Allah.'

And now he moves to the Aga and he picks up the matches and you see what he's going to do.

'Mohammed – don't.'

'But I have failed my mullah, I have failed my cause. Goodbye.'

He strikes the match.

'But Mohammed, I love you, I love you, I love you with all my heart more than Troy, more than the Towers, your strength your mystery your heart. I – Let's run away now, before the security forces . . . Let's begin again, there's a cottage, the countryside – '

'No. I have loved you, Amy. But we are just people.'

'That's all there is. People. Lonely, wounded people and their loving hearts.'

'No. There is Destiny, there is Allah's will, there is the Cause. And all of these are bigger than people. I pity you, my love, in your small world of people. No purpose . . . How do you live with this? My sadness is with you.'

He looks up.

'Oh please, Allah, let your servant come to Paradise.'

And then – woosh – he's alight, the flame racing across his body and his skin and hair and crackling and the smell is almost sweet in your converted abbatoir.

And then you – this feeling deep within and you call out:

'Oh take me, take me, Mohammed. Take me in those arms. I love you. I don't know you. I'll never know you. I will never believe a thing you believe. But fold me in your burning arms, press your flaming chest against me, scorch me with your groin of fire.

Then, as if in slow motion – fuck it, we are in slow motion – you run toward the burning man.

And now – a life avoiding, avoiding, afraid of death (character notes: your mother's cancer, your best friend's suicide, your father dwindling into Alzheimered oblivion), all your life scared and your denial of death and now the freedom, the total exhilirating three-dimensional freedom as you call on the Angel of Death to take you and –

'Yes, Mohammed. Yeeeeessss!'

And you're closing in on him, you're reaching him, your hair is starting to crack and sizzle as the flames are inches from you and then, then, then, your arms enfold him and his skin begins to melt onto yours:

'Yeeessssss!'

And then there's the crack of glass – do you know Liz? Fabulous little dyke, gonna be doing all your stunts? – the crack of glass as you both fall and fall and fall, four storeys and into the pool below.

Underwater those bodies, twisting around, the flames becoming smoke, becoming charred and sodden, your bodies twisting one over the other.

Until you come up – eighty-degree burns on his part, twenty degrees for you but –

There's love, like a great wave of release, suddenly there's love, there in the pool there's love and you kiss and caress and you fuck in the water, the pleasure of the lovemaking, the pain of the burns all rolling into one.

But then they're there. The Feds, the cops, the special ops – all the special forces of the world – and they pull Mohammed from your arms and you're screaming:

'Please I love him. You have to – love will conquer this. I know it. Yes there is terror and horror and he's done wickedness, yes – but we've found love here tonight and I – '

Your final vision. Your final vision of Mohammed – the body a mass of burns, the smell of chlorine, the feel of him still inside you – a vision as the butt of a gun pushes you to the ground and the doors of the van open, the savage barking of a dog, the manacles clipping around the hands and feet of this man you love.

You rush into the street – you throw yourself into the path of the van – you are on the verge of madness now – I'd love to see you play the verge of madness – you block the path of the van – surely they must stop for you? – but the van is racing toward you – at the last moment your nerve cracks and – wham! – you throw yourself out of the way.

Your cowardice. How you despise your cowardice. When an eighteen-year-old boy can blow himself up, why can't you stand in front of a racing vehicle to save the man you love?

You pick yourself up from the pavement with difficulty. Already the bruising is beginning. You see the TV crew, the redhead with the microphone running towards you in the night and you're very wet and very cold and very alone.

No. He isn't a bad man, you tell the News. He is a good man and I love him.

And then your stomach loops, your knees disappear and you lose consciousness.

You're out for a couple of days. Your mother cares for you. Your mother or a neighbour or an aunt or blah blah blah. She's a mentor, okay? Too old to fuck, too old to kick ass, but we have a place for her in our world.

And this wise old woman, this woman whose sexuality has died so that she might think of higher things, this woman says:

'Hush now, child, hush. You must forget him. You must let Mohammed go. There is a time for everything and your time for Mohammed has ended and now is the time to live a new life.'

And you look up from the bed and you feel the warmth of her wisdom and you say:

'Yes MotherAuntNeighbour yes.'

And so there is an emptiness. An emptiness which once he filled. And your life begins again. You begin to spin around the globe again. There's the constant drive drive drive to outsource customer relations to expanding economies. There are several weeks in China.

And back at home Nathan gets in touch again. Nathan who loved you at school. Nathan who married the fitness instructor but lost her in the rail crash. Nathan who has loved you all the time.

And you sit in sushi bars and theatres and taxis with Nathan and he holds your hand and he touches your knee and all the time he's telling you what a special person you are but really there is nothing that you hear.

And you take Nathan in your mouth. You take his broad beautiful cock in your mouth and you force it back and back into you so that you gag because when you gag you know you'll feel something. But you don't feel anything.

And you plead with Nathan to hit you about the head. You put the club in his hand and say: 'Come on, come on, strike me.' But he loves you in such a tender way and he runs into the night and that's Nathan gone.

You hang about the coach station and you pull up your skirt for teenagers in toilets and in alleyways – looking for a smell that will drown the scent of Mohammed.

(This is edgy, okay? This is fucking – fucking edgy stuff, okay? What do you think? What are you thinking? I'd love a word here. Just a word to let me know how I'm . . .

I'm pitching my bollocks off and that –

I like it. I like it. Enjoy your power. I would. If I had that power then I would use it.

You bitch, you bitch. I love you, you bitch. Respect to the bitch.

No stay stay stay. Stay. Hear the end of the story. Hear the end of the story or I'll . . .

Thank you.)

It's a bar. A bar with a TV screen. A fucking scuzzy prostitutes-and-drunkards bar by the coach station when you first see the images of Mohammed on the TV screen. They've been smuggled out of the offshore prison. It's a blurry image – nothing more than a grey shadow moving across the TV screen. But you know straight away. You know the man you love as he is dragged across the screen, the hair torn from his scalp. And you see her apply the electrodes to his testicles, you see the dignity in his face as the other guards laugh and jeer, you see the spit on his face, then his body dancing as the electrodes burn at the testes you have held so often in the night.

You sit in your fabulous loft-style apartment that evening and you watch that image played over as it rolls through the news and you listen to the experts and the politicians and the lawyers and the celebrities trying to give it their story, every time a new story as once again the electrodes are clipped onto Mohammed's sac, as the spit hits his face, the jeers and the jaunts and then the electricity dancing through his body.

And, just as suddenly as the power jolts through your lover, the resolve jolts through you. You leap from your chair, you throw your towel to the ground and you turn your naked body to the screen and you call out:

'Hold on. Hold on. Because I'm coming, I'm coming to save you – lover.'

And we crane, crane, crane as though the gods, the heavens, the eternal powers hear and endorse your cry.

A montage. You're training. A boy's boxing club in the east of the city where you push yourself until your eyes swell with blood. The icy lake where you swim for hours before even the ducks are awake. The Tibetan monastery where you learn to breathe and kick and chop. The mountain state where your Kalashnikov is slung across your breast ready to fire as the targets go flying into the sky.

And as one image melts to another, we see Amy disappearing from view. She's gone. Amy – who once lived on coffee and air-miles and longing – Amy – who never found the perfect diet, never found the perfect man, never found a therapist she could trust – this Amy is ripped away to reveal a creature of muscle and will and strength.

You are hero. Before you, we are nothing. Before you, we – oh saviour, oh saviour, oh saviour.

If only you would save me, if only – this story were . . . there is an inner truth to this st . . . but . . . it's what we would want to . . .

No. You're right. Fucking pointless. I'm fucking pointless. What is this piece of crap? What is this . . . ? What is this story? What's this . . . three mil on an opening weekend? What is that? It's shit.

So you don't . . . have to . . .

I'll call a car . . .

(*To phone.*) A car for . . . yeah, yeah . . . account.

Thank you. Thank you. Thank you.

Listen, just . . .

There's just this . . . okay?

That final night in your fabulous loft-style apartment
that was once an abbatoir. And in your fabulous apartment
you take Mohammed's mat from the floor and you bless
it and you place the mat in your rucksack and you take
Mohammed's knife and you kiss the blade and you slip the
knife amongst the weapons that are slung about your waist.

And then we cut to –

Boom! The explosion crashes open the door to the corridor
and in you come – a fury in fatigues.

'Where is he? Where is he?' you scream at the Cuban guard
pushing him against the wall. 'Where the fuck is he?'

And your fist – crack crack crack – against the Cuban's
skull.

'I'm coming to fucking find you,' you scream, blasting at the
guards who come running toward you. Your bullets tear
into them and hurtle them against the walls and the blood
begins to run in rivers down the corridors of Uncle Sam's
detention centre.

'Mohammed! Mohammed! Mohammed!'

Boom! You blow open the doors to the first cell and out they
come the men and women in their orange jumpsuits,
blinking into the light and calling to Allah as they dance
with their liberty.

But he's not there. So many faces – but not the face of the
man you love.

You blow open the second door, the third door, the fourth
door – and they are pouring down the corridors of the
prison now, a great carnival of the enchained.

There he is! Mohammed! You run towards him, you throw yourself towards him, you pull at his shoulder –

'Please?'

The stranger is terrified at this fierce warrior who is clinging to him.

So. The search goes on and you go into the lift and down and down and down – until . . .

The light is dim here. Many floors above the orange jumpsuits and the guards are fighting, but here there's not a sound. 'Pad like the cat, strike like the tiger,' said the Tibetan monk and so you pad through the dimness – and strike like the tiger as the guard turns the corner, slitting his throat with one keen slice from Mohammed's blade.

And finally the silhouette against the bars. And he's weeping.

'Oh Mohammed.'

The hair has been pulled from his skull, he's burnt, he's bruised and –

'Amy?'

'Yes, Mohammed.'

'Go. I won't see you.'

'Please – '

'Western bitch who destroyed my bond to Allah.'

'Mohammed.'

'Western bitch who defiled my body and tore at my heart.'

'Mohammed.'

'Western bitch who cannot see Paradise.'

'Please, Mohammed. I have been . . . there was Amy and I spit on her. I spit on her restless, pointless, aching decadence. Yes, I spit. I spit – and I pray to be reborn – reborn in Allah's eye and I will not rest until this world is purged of the infidel and all stand pure before Allah – together we will do this, my love, we will fight and struggle and work until this hollow world is purified and all are ready for Paradise.'

'This prison is hell.'

'And I have come to take you back. Please, Mohammed, let me . . . '

'Yes, my love.'

And so you blast open the bars and out he steps, the broken figure of this man you love. And how gently you hold him in that moment. And how tender but how lingering is that kiss as your souls melt into one.

(There will be awards for this, there will be prizes – but let's not sully . . .)

'Come,' you tell Mohammed, and you lead him down the corridor, but –

Tuh! The lone guard – you take her out, but not before her bullet ricochets around the walls and – slow, slow, slow motion drills its way into Mohammed's head. He crumples – slow – and – slow – the blood stutters from his mouth and ears.

There is no God, no angels, no nothing in our world but still . . .

There is actually a moment. We're going to need a fantastic lighting-cameraman, but there is actually a moment when the soul leaves the body. Have you ever . . . ? I've seen it. I've seen it and, erm – if we can get that on celluloid then . . . they can fucking kiss my arse.

So Mohammed's soul leaves his body for Paradise.

And you mourn him and you mature in that moment – not in a gradual – bereavement matures you in a moment.

And you see it's all screens and show and display and symbols and acting make-believe emptiness.

And you pull out the knife and you feel the weight of the knife in your hand and the sharpness of the blade and you turn the blade toward you, oh to do it, to do it, to do it, just to feel the dignity of Ancient Rome.–

But then –

Cut to your POV.

And it's the rucksack with the prayer mat.

And you take out the prayer mat. And you play: The knife or the prayer mat? Prayer mat or the knife. Which will it be? Which will you . . . ?

Knife. Prayer mat. Face. Knife. Prayer mat. Face.

And then . . . you put down the knife. You don't kill yourself.

And you move across the floor and you reach the prayer mat and you look around – unsure which way to position yourself – but then –

A sudden swell of certainty – you're underscored – and then you kneel down, you kneel down upon the mat and – she's a great character:

'Allah? I will revenge, Allah.'

Thank you for listening. Thank you for coming here. It's been a privilege to tell the story. And you, if you want to go back to your, you know, manager and agent and PR and your people and, you know, take the piss, use the script to . . . then fine, fine, because at least I've told you, I have told you.

Exit **Olivia**. **James** *phones*.

Hey! Loved it. Loved it. She loved it.

The Cut

The Cut premiered at the Donmar Warehouse, London, on 23 February 2006. The cast was as follows:

Paul	Ian McKellen
John	Jimmy Akingbola
Gita	Bindu de Stoppani
Susan	Deborah Findlay
Mina	Emma Beattie
Stephen	Tom Burke

Director	Michael Grandage
Designer	Paul Wills
Lighting Designer	Paule Constable
Music and Sound Score	Adam Cork

Characters

Scene One	**Paul**
	John
	Gita
Scene Two	**Paul**
	Susan
	Mina
Scene Three	**Paul**
	Stephen

Scene One

A room. A desk. **Paul** *and* **John**.

Paul   Were the searches made?

John   I was searched, yes.

Paul   Was there any unnecessary brutality?

John   No. No, I wouldn't say it was unnecessary brutality.

Paul   Because I need to record any cases of unnecessary . . .
I'm compiling a dossier. Which many people are eager to read.

John   I see.

Paul   The last lot were very slack on unnecessary brutality.
Blind eyes were turned. You remember?

John   Yes.

Paul   But we intend to be different. We're shining a light
on . . . We're coming down, very hard. You see? On
unnecessary . . .

John   Yes.

Paul   But we need the figures, so if you were in any way . . .

John   No, no.

Paul   You have to tell me.

John   No.

Paul   Look, to you I know I'm – what? – I'm Authority.
Power. Strength. The Father.

John   Well –

Paul   But honestly you must tell me if there was any
unnecessary – for the dossier.

John   No.

Paul   You're quite sure?

John   Very sure.

Paul   Well, that's good. Good. Good. No fist?

John   No.

Paul   No boot?

John   No.

Paul   Good. Good. Good.

Beat.

You were searched?

John   Yes.

Paul   Thoroughly?

John   Yes.

Paul   But in such a way as not to . . .

John   Yes, yes, yes.

Paul   Good, good, good. You understand why we have to . . . ?

John   Of course.

Paul   Someone did actually pull a gun on me recently. Little bastard actually got a gun through and pulled it out on me.

John   Shit.

Paul   And fired.

John   Shit.

Paul   I actually saw the bullet coming out of the gun, saw it coming towards me and ducked. Just in time.

John   Shit.

Paul   So as you can imagine I gave those guys out there merry hell. 'Security? Security? Call yourself Security and you let some fucker through with a gun?' We've had to set a new target for performance. Utterly thorough without any unnecessary brutality. Using that performance indicator, how would you say the operatives did? In your experience?

John   Well . . .

Paul   Excellentverygoodgoodaveragepoor?

John   Very good.

Paul   So – some room for improvement. But . . . getting there. Good.

He records this in a file.

Now. Can I give you any more information?

John   No. I don't think so.

Paul   You've read the leaflets?

John   I've read everything.

Paul   Well . . . good, good. Very . . . impressive.

John   I've been preparing for this moment for a long time. Books. The clips. I've thought about this.

Paul   Good.

John   I wanted to be ready.

Paul   Excellent.

John   I really wanted to be ready for the Cut.

Paul   Yes. Yes. Well, we'll have to see if . . .

John   Where are the instruments?

Paul   They're with –

John   Only in the clips they have the instruments all laid out, you know. On the desk. There. Before I . . . before he . . . walks into the room they're all laid out and then, 'Are you ready for the Cut?' 'Yes.' And – instruments in and –

Paul   Pain.

John   Pain and then – done.

Paul   Yes, well – that was the last lot. All very brutal. All very fast. We're . . . different.

John   Yes?

Paul   Oh yes. We're very different. We've made some changes.

John   Oh. I see.

Paul   We're a force for change. So . . . let's consider some other options.

John   No.

Paul   We're going to look at –

John   No.

Paul   No?

John   I want to . . . I'm here for the Cut. I want the Cut. That's what I'm here for. The Cut.

Paul   And I'm here to look at the options. And as I'm . . . as I'm this side of the desk, we're going to look at the options. We're going to look at your choices. Alright?

John   Alright.

Paul   There's a prison facility. We offer a prison facility to the insane. Are you insane?

John   No.

Paul   Because if you're insane –

John   I'm not insane.

Paul   Although prison doesn't come cheap. You pay. Or – poverty pending – we pay. So nobody's keen on the prison facility. Still, if you're actually insane –

John   I'm not.

Paul   Do you have the paperwork?

John   Here.

He hands **Paul** *a piece of paper.*

Paul   Well, this all seems to be . . . so you're actually sane?

John   Yes.

Paul   Well, that's very impressive. In this day and age. Now, there's the army. Let's think about that.

John   No.

Paul   Or the university. Maybe we should be sending you to the university.

John   No, no. I don't want –

Paul   The army and the university. Much more cost-efficient than prison. Let's talk about –

John   No, no, let's not. Let's not mess about.

Paul   Mess about?

John   Mess about. This, this, this . . . you're the man who does the Cut, right?

Paul   I'm in the office of the building where the Cut is –

John   Then do the Cut. Do the Cut on me.

Paul   This is the office. This is the building. But that doesn't have to define . . . me. You. We have choices. You and me. We can be . . . there's the army, the university, the prison. So much choice.

John   No, no.

Paul   Oh, oh, would you rather be under the last lot?

John   No, no, no.

Paul   Because if you're telling me you'd rather be under the last lot then that, my son, is a political statement, and if you're making political statements, if you're standing here in a public place – and yes, this is classified as a public place –

standing in a public space and making political statements
then it's the university for you. I'll send you straight off to the
university and they'll soon put a stop to these political
statements.

John   No, no, no. I wasn't . . . there wasn't anything
political, just . . .

Paul   Yes?

John   . . . just I've got this far, you know?

Paul   Of course.

John   Always another office, always another interview,
another search, another form to fill. From my village to the
town to the city, and now . . . now that I've got this far, I
thought you'd just . . . just . . .

Paul   Yes?

John   I thought you were a rubber stamp.

Paul   I am more, I am much much much more than a
rubber as you put it stamp.

John   Of course.

Paul   Would I have all this space, all this facility, all this . . .
fucking impressive . . . How do I look to you . . . ?

John   Well, yes, impressive.

Paul   And?

John   And, and . . .

Paul   And?

John   Old. As in wise. As in responsible. As in, as in, as in,
as in . . .

Paul   Authority.

John   Authoritative.

Paul As in authoritative authority. Yes. As in burdened with, the burden of . . .

John Exactly.

Paul Do you think I tell my wife what I do here? (I have a wife.) Do you think my children . . . ? (One's in prison — expensive — one's in university — cheaper.) Do you think I tell my children what I do here? Have you thought about that?

John Well, maybe you should. Maybe you should. Maybe. Because, listen, the Cut, I think it's . . . I want the Cut. I think the Cut's a very beautiful . . . a very old and beautiful . . . it's a ritual, a custom, something we . . .

Paul I don't think so.

John To actually leave your body.

Paul Have you any idea of the suffering? The pain? The great screams as the instruments go in?

John Of course.

Paul They claw at me. They howl at the sky. It's barbaric.

John I know all that. All the clips. But I want —

Paul And I have to carry all this on. Disgusting. You know we actually — off the record — have a working party looking at, considering ending the whole thing.

John No.

Paul Off the record.

John Why?

Paul Progress. Humanity. Etcetera. Our core values.

John But that's centuries of . . . you can't wipe out centuries of . . . my grandmother, my uncles, so many centuries —

Paul You can't stand in the way of core values. None of us can.

John   Everybody had the Cut.

Paul   And for now of course we're carrying it through.

John   Good.

Paul   Just . . . softening the blow. Talking. We get to know you. You get to know us.

John   How does that . . . ?

Paul   For the records.

John   Please. I'd like to see the instruments. I don't want to talk.

Paul   I'll be the judge –

John   This isn't right. This isn't how it's supposed to be. I'm not supposed to get to know you. You're not supposed to talk to me. You're just supposed to show me the instruments.

Paul   New procedures.

John   I haven't heard about –

Paul   There's new procedures all the time. Every day practically. Only this morning I received a directive.

John   Where do you keep the instruments?

Paul   New guidelines for talking. Keep things inclusive.

John   I don't want to talk.

Paul   If you want to see the directive –

John   I'm not going to talk.

Paul   Box files full of the things. Aims. Objectives. Targets. Outcomes. Let me show them. We're very open. It's a root and branch thing.

John   No, no, no. Just – Cut me. Come on. Do it. Do it. Show me the instruments. Get the instruments and Cut me.

Paul   Just – like that – cruel, cold, hard, impersonal?

John   Yes, yes, yes.

Paul   That would make me very unhappy. You'd be in great pain –

John   I know that.

Paul   But also I'd be in great pain. Inside. Enormous pain – physical for you, spiritual for me.

John   Yes. Please. Come on. It's what I want. Fuck's sake – that's what I want.

Paul   Are you sure you're not insane?

John   You've seen the –

Paul   And I suppose we'll have to take their word, but still I've never seen anybody so . . . keen.

John   Yes, well . . .

Paul   So keen for the Cut. Why are you – ?

John   I don't want to talk.

Paul   Just a little longer.

John   I'd rather we just –

Paul   Tell me. Tell me and I'll show you the instruments.

John   You've got them?

Paul   Of course I've got them. Couldn't be in my position unless I had the instruments, could I?

John   Then where . . . ?

Paul   Ah.

John   In the desk? There's a special drawer in the – ?

Paul   No. Stuffed to the brim with directives. The girl. The girl has the instruments.

John   The girl?

Paul   Gita. Did you see Gita on your way in?

John   No.

Paul   Well yes, easily missed, Gita. Can't speak. Can't hear. It's a condition. But we found her a place. Inclusion.

John   Tell her to bring the instruments in.

Paul   She may be –

John   Tell her to bring the instrument or I won't talk.

Paul *goes to a door, opens it, beckons.*

Enter **Gita**.

Paul   You're looking very good today, Gita. We're almost ready. We've almost finished talking and we're almost ready for the instruments. Could you get them ready, Gita? Thank you.

Exit **Gita**.

Paul   She's very good. Back in a minute. So – tell me. Tell me why you're so different.

John   Am I?

Paul   Oh yes. Totally different. I've never seen . . . Normally I see fear, anger. Sometimes . . . sullen, nothing. But you're keen. Because . . . ?

John   Because. Because I want to be free. Free of, of, of me. Of all this. I want it to be Cut away. I want to be Cut away from this body. Yes – and this history and this wanting and this busyness and this schooling and these, these ties. I want to be released.

Paul   And you think – ? You really think?

John   Yes, yes.

Paul   You think that's what the Cut – ?

John   I know. I know that's what the Cut does.

Paul   You're very idealistic.

John   I don't think so.

Paul   Bit of a dreamer.

John   No.

Paul   Yes, dreamer. Because, look . . . wouldn't we all? Wouldn't we all like – ?

John   We can.

Paul   We'd all like to be free. Believe me, I want to be free of bodies, of history, of wanting . . . I'd like that just as much as . . .

John   Then . . . free yourself.

Paul   I can't.

John   You can. Anybody can.

Paul   No. No. I Cut. You are Cut. That's my burden. Nobody's ever changed that –

John   But if you –

Paul   We can stop Cutting. But we'll still be the people who used to Cut. You'll still be the people who used to be Cut. Always the same. No fucking point. We soften the blow. Maybe we end the Cut. But still the old circles, the old divides. Young and I thought – change it all. I can make it all better. Nothing's going to be the same. Out with the last lot. And now look at me. Repellent. Can't tell my beautiful wife, my beautiful children –

John   Listen, listen, listen.

Paul   What does it matter? Send my beautiful children to the prison or the university, still they'll be . . .

John   Listen to me.

Paul   They'll always be Cutters, never Cut.

John   I want to show you.

Paul   The old lot, the new lot. Everything's the same.
We've changed nothing.

John   Ssssh. Ssssh. I've got something to show you.

Paul   Yes?

John   Yes. I've discovered . . . I want to share . . . I always
knew what the Cut was going to be, okay?

Paul   Alright.

John   Liberty. Freedom. Nothingness. I knew that. Don't
ask me how. But from dot I knew, so I . . .

Paul   Yes?

John   Prepared myself. Practised little moments of
emptiness. Not for ever like the Cut but moments. And you
can do that.

Paul   I can't.

John   You can. Each of us can. Each and every one of us
can free ourselves.

Paul   Not me.

John   If only you'll . . . shut your eyes.

Paul   No.

John   Please.

Paul   No. I'm sorry. But you understand. After the incident.
With the gun. After the incident with the gun I find trust
impossible.

John   Of course.

Paul   Which has made lovemaking with my wife, which has
made it – does this embarrass you?

John   No, no.

Paul   Which has made lovemaking with my wife impossible.
It's only when you can't . . . when you can no longer close

your eyes during the, the, the . . . act that you realise . . .
lovemaking with the eyes wide open . . . impossible.

John I see.

Paul Unnerving for her, embarrassing for me.

John Of course. I've been searched.

Paul But if you strangled me.

John Beat me away. Beat me to the ground. Beat me to
death. I'm weak. You're strong. You can easily beat me.

Paul Yes, yes, I suppose I can.

John But I'm not going to strangle you.

Paul No?

John No. Now please. The eyes.

Paul *closes his eyes.*

Long silence.

John And there's total darkness.

Paul Well, almost.

John Please don't speak. That's vital. It's vital that you
don't speak.

Paul I understand.

John Ah-hah. Total darkness. And you have no body. Your
body has dissolved. Dissolved or melted away. Every piece of
skin or bone or hair. Every last cell gone away. The cage has
vanished. And you are free.

Feel the darkness. Feel the void.

Remember how they used to scare you with that? Remember
then how you used to scare yourself with that?

The darkness. Where the monsters live. Where the witches
live. Where the paedophiles are. The darkness. Don't go into

the darkness. Carry the candle. Leave a light in the window. Take a torch into the woods.

Lies. All of it lies.

The void. It'll eat you up. The chasm that swallows the sailors, swallows the ships, swallows the astronauts. The hole, the pit, the gap. Avoid. Avoid. Avoid. Take a map, make a rope bridge. Steer clear of the void.

Lies lies, all of it lies.

They've told you lies and you've kept your eyes open. When all freedom asked of you was to close your eyes.

And now you've closed them. And you've made a start.

But still you're trying to work out where the light switch is. Still the torch is in your hand. Still you're fingering the switch. In case. In case. In case.

Don't. Please. I beg you. Spin around. Spin around until you're dizzy and there's no light switch. Let the torch fall from your hand. Let it roll away into the forest. Let the mud suck it up and rot it away.

And stand in the darkness. And become the darkness.

The truth.

And feel everything go.

There's no history. All that struggling to move forward, to expand, to progress. That's gone away.

And there's no society. All the prisons and the universities have fallen down or been exploded. Or maybe they never were. It doesn't matter.

The truth.

And your wife and your children. Eaten away by cancers or burnt to nothing or maybe never born. Generation after generation never born. Back and back until the first stroke of the first day of the first time. None of it ever was.

The truth.

And so there's nothing.

Don't fight. Don't try and feel your body. Don't reach for the reports. Don't try and call your wife.

Because it's all nothing.

There's only truth. There's only you.

Darkness is light. Void is everything. You are truth.

Long silence.

And open your eyes.

And open your eyes.

And open your eyes.

Paul   I don't want to.

John   Open them.

Paul   No.

John   I've got a gun. In my hand. Pointing at you. I'm squeezing the trigger.

Paul *opens his eyes.*

John   Sorry. I had to –

Paul   No gun? No gun? Where's the fucking gun? You said there was a –

John   Yes, because you wouldn't –

Paul   Listen, son, don't fuck around. If there's a gun then have a fucking gun, okay? Okay? Okay?

John   I was just trying –

Paul   Fuck. I wanted to . . . I didn't want to open my . . . why did you make . . . ?

John   Because it's not healthy.

Paul   Healthy? Healthy? Healthy? Fuck you. Fuck you.
Fuck you. Sorry. Sorry. Sorry.

Pause.

I'm sorry. I really wanted . . . I just wanted you to shoot . . .

John   It was a tactic.

Paul   Really thought you'd shoot me. That's what I wanted.
I wanted to be shot with my eyes shut.

John   I wouldn't do that.

Paul   But then – cunt that I am – I opened my eyes. Fucked
up. Because I'm – what? – a coward. And you – cunt – no
gun. We're both cunts. Everyone's cunts. Everything's a cunt.
The whole shebang is one big fucking cunting cunty cunt.

John   No, no.

Paul   Because that's what you're . . . preaching, isn't it? In
your . . . sermon.

John   I don't use words like that.

Paul   But you are. That's what you're saying. Everything's
shit. Everything's fucked up. There's nothing worth crap.

John   No, no.

Paul   We've tried everything and it's all a void. That's what
you said.

John   No I didn't. No I didn't.

Paul   Yes you did. Please don't correct me. I know. I know.
What were you doing? Talking. Blah. Blah. Blah. But I, I was
listening. With my eyes shut. And I know what I heard.

John   From your perspective.

Paul   The truth. Everything's finished. Everything's over.
We're all done.

John   You're twisting everything –

Paul   Listen son. I'm old. I'm wise. You gibber. I shift the shit and pick out the gems. Okay? Okay? Okay?

John   Okay.

Paul   And you're right. And I admire you. I revere you. To say what's been in my head, what I've never been able to . . . the articulation. Because, as you said, I was afraid and I have been lied to. For generations.

And there in the dark. In the moment. I saw. I'm worthless.

I'm a piece of shit. I'm a speck of shit on a lump of shit on a piece of shit. I'm nothing.

And I don't want to carry on.

And I do have . . .

He produces a gun.

Shoot me.

John   No.

Paul   As an act of kindness.

John   No. I'm not an emotional –

Paul   Yes, yes, yes. Go. Off you go.

John   No.

Paul   It's going to get very bloody in here. I'm going for the head. Blood and brains all over the place. And I don't want you to be a part of that.

John   You mustn't.

Paul   Here. I'll stamp your report. Show it to the girl on the desk. She'll give you your travel money home. We pay reasonable second class fares. Go back to your village – I take it you have a village and a – and a family.

John   No.

Paul Alright. You might want to stand back. Blood in your hair and so on.

John Don't be so . . . don't be so . . . no, no, no. I'm here. I'm here for the Cut. That's what I'm here for. That's what you're supposed to do. You're supposed to administer the Cut.

Paul I'm supposed to . . .

John That's your duty. That's your calling. That's why you were chosen.

Paul Yes, well, I'm . . .

John And that's why I'm here. That's what I've waited so long for. This is what I've been planning for.

Paul I'm sorry. Things change.

John No, no, no. The clips, the books, waiting, waiting, planning, planning. Every moment I ever lived for this moment, you can't oh please oh please oh please oh please oh please . . .

Paul There's a tear.

John Yes.

Paul You've got a tear.

John Yes.

Paul That's very emotional . . .

John I know. Sorry. Sorry. Where's Gita? Where are the instruments?

Paul They're being sterilised.

John Please. Bring them in.

Paul We have to reuse them. Public finances. But also sterilise them. Public health.

John I understand. Please. Show me the instruments.

Paul   You're a very selfish young man.

John   Yes.

Paul   To ride roughshod over my suffering.

John   I know, I know.

Paul   Have you any idea of the burden for a man – of my class?

John   No.

Paul   No, no, you don't. Very well.

He rings a bell.

John   Thank you.

Paul   This evening I shall drive my wife to the university. She's made a fruit cake. Our son is reading Advanced Politics. But he still enjoys his fruit cake. And I shall watch her handing over the fruit cake. But all the time I'll be suffering. Like nobody can believe. And I'll wake up tomorrow. And I'll say: today I'll shoot myself. That kid who got the Cut was right. I should shoot myself.

John   Are the instruments . . . ?

Paul   Coming. The kid was right. I should shoot myself. But I won't. Oh, I'll look at the gun. I'll handle it. All day long under the desk I'll be handling the gun. But I won't fire. I won't fire tomorrow or the next day or the next day or the next day or the next day. Or never. I'll be permanently not shooting myself. Can you imagine the horror of that? No you can't. Of course you can't. You – you – you . . . shit.

*Enter **Gita**, carrying the instruments.*

Paul   Ah, Gita, thank you, thank you. Gita's just joined us. She's still training but she's doing very well. Down there, Gita.

Gita *places the instruments down and steps back.*

John   Can I touch them?

Paul Well, it's not a regular . . .

John Please.

Paul Of course. No, no, Gita. It's alright. Stay.

John *picks up the instruments.*

John These are . . . twenty-three years old.

Paul Public finances. Lack of investment.

John From a workshop in the north. The northwestern workshop.

Paul Very impressive.

John Look at them. Just look.

Paul I'm afraid they're purely functional to me.

John No, no, no. Classic craftsmanship. This is an honour. Thank you. Thank you.

Paul Shall we get on with it?

John Yes.

Paul Gita.

Gita *comes forward.*

Paul I envy you. I envy everything about you. If you could give me a word. Just a word so I can shoot myself.

John No.

Paul You've broken me.

John I didn't mean to.

Paul That doesn't make it any fucking better. Gita. The lights.

Gita *switches off the lights. Total darkness.*

Paul You are here for the Cut. Please prepare yourself for the Cut.

Long, long pause.

Paul   I don't want to . . .

John   You have to.

Paul   Please, I can't . . .

John   Now. Do it now.

Paul   Fuck it. Fuck it. Fuck it. The Cut is about to take place.

Long, long pause. **John** *gasps as the instruments go in.*

John   Thank you. Thank you. Thank you.

Scene Two

Paul's *flat.* **Paul** *and* **Susan**.

Susan   She's like a child. Quite honestly like a simple little child. I walk in and she's looking at it boiling over. Actually standing there and watching – just . . . watching as it's boiling over. And I say, 'Mina – the milk's boiling over,' and she says, 'Yes, Miss,' and then she carries on, carries on looking.

Paul   Mmm.

Susan   And I suppose I should have been angry. I suppose angry would have been an altogether appropriate response. Would you have been angry?

Paul   Well . . .

Susan   I think you might have been. I think you might have flown into one of your rages.

Paul   Well . . .

Susan   Oh yes, I can see you now tearing into her. Just tearing straight into her.

Paul   I don't know.

Susan   But somehow I . . . I . . . I smiled, maybe – I think I laughed a bit, I indulged . . . yes, alright, I indulged . . . and I said, 'Maybe if you turned down the . . . you see?'

Paul   Mmmmmmm . . .

Susan   And she did. She did when I actually told her what to do.

Paul   Well good.

Susan   But of course tomorrow we'll be right back to square one. She'll be watching it boil over all over again. Little goldfish.

Paul   Yes.

Susan   It's a great pressure on me. This watching. All the time watching, guiding. There's a burden.

Paul   Of course.

Susan   Sometimes half an hour with her . . . I have to lie down. In the dark. For several hours.

Paul   We could have her reassigned.

Susan   I went to the hospital.

Paul   Shall I look into having her reassigned?

Susan   I went to the hospital. But really I was fobbed off. A few tablets. They're useless.

Paul   Let's get her reassigned.

Susan   And can you imagine the fuss?

Paul   There needn't be a fuss.

Susan   You haven't seen the family. You're never here when the . . . Oh, there's a father. And a mother. And a brother. I suspect that she has a child.

Paul   Really?

Susan   I suspect. Just a . . . And they'll all be round here crying and pleading and looking and . . .

Paul   Really? Really? Really?

Susan   You don't know. You just don't know. Oh yes. I don't think I can handle the fuss.

Paul   So we'll keep her?

Susan   I don't know. I don't know. I suppose. I suppose we must. I suppose I'll just have to do the best I can.

Paul   You're a remarkable person.

Susan   Thank you.

Paul   No. I mean it. You're a remarkable person. And I appreciate what you do. For us.

Susan   Supper will be late.

Paul   I just want you to know . . . you're valued.

Susan   After the milk and everything . . . there'll be a wait for supper.

Paul   Ah well.

Susan   So just try . . . try not to get angry until the food arrives.

Paul   I'm not going to . . .

Susan   I know you, I know you. Your blood sugar . . . if the blood sugar's not even that's when you start to get . . .

Paul   What? What?

Susan   You get tetchy.

Paul   No, no, no.

Susan   It's always the same. Yes, yes, yes. You're always the same. So just hold on.

Paul   You know me.

Susan   Oh yes.

Paul   You know me very well.

Susan   I know you totally.

Paul   Ah.

Susan   I know you absolutely and totally.

Paul   Yes. Yes. Is that boring?

Susan   Darling . . .

Paul   A man with no secrets?

Susan   Darling.

Paul   Is it dull to have no doors left to open?

Susan   It's . . . comfortable. I'd say we're comfortable. Wouldn't you say we're comfortable?

Paul   Yes.

Susan   Yes. Comfortable's the word.

Paul   But physically . . .

Susan   You know there's a big push now. From the universities. I got a letter from Stephen.

Paul   Mmm?

Susan   Today. Stephen wrote from the university. He's looking forward to his fruit cake. Stephen wrote and he said there's a big push now in the universities. The students mainly. But also the lecturers. And there's a big push against the Cut.

Paul   Really?

Susan   Yes. That's what he said.

Paul   Really?

Susan   Yes. There's a real groundswell of . . . there's a real mood for ending the whole thing.

Paul   Really?

Susan   What do you think?

Paul   If that's what Stephen –

Susan   Yes. But what do you think?

Paul   I think, I think –

Susan   I think they're right. I think they're absolutely . . .

Paul   Really? Really?

Susan   I think these reforms, these, these, these new criteria
. . . I mean softening the blow I think that's . . . I think that's .
. . dressing . . . and I think it's time . . .

Paul   What's he doing?

Susan   Mmm?

Paul   What's Stephen . . . ?

Susan   I don't . . . writing . . . stuff . . . they have papers
and . . . discussions and . . . I don't . . .

Paul   So . . . talking?

Susan   Talking and writing. Yes. Yes.

Paul   Ah, ah, ah, ah. Student stuff.

Susan   It's a start.

Paul   Is it? Is it? Is it?

Susan   Shall I hurry her along?

Paul   What?

Susan   Mina. Shall I hurry her along?

Paul   Why?

Susan   You're getting tetchy. It's starting.

Paul   No.

Susan   I can see it. The blood sugar's . . . dropping. There's a . . . you're starting to snap.

Paul   No. No. It's just . . . politics.

Susan   Yes?

Paul   It makes me uncomfortable.

Susan   I'm sorry.

Paul   No. No. But I've . . . I've had a day.

Susan   Of course.

Paul   I've had a day and all I wanted was to get back to you and sit with you and eat and read and . . .

Susan   Talk.

Paul   And talk, yes, of course talk and so of course I find it uncomfortable . . .

Susan   Of course. What did you do?

Paul   Mmm?

Susan   What did you do today?

Paul   Oh. Nothing.

Susan   You always say . . . Really? Really? Nothing?

Paul   Well nothing of . . . numbers, figures, reports, dossiers.

Susan   Ah.

Paul   I've got a title. I've got an office. I've got a big office. But really, really I'm just a rubber stamp.

Susan   No, darling.

Paul   Yes, really.

Susan   No, darling. I'm sure . . . I know you're much much much more than a rubber stamp.

Paul   No.

Susan I try to imagine what you do. I try to picture it. I lie on my bed in the dark in the afternoon. And Mina is breaking something. She's always breaking something in the next room. And I try to block her out. It's better now I've got the pills. And I block her out and I try to picture what you're doing.

Paul Really?

Susan Really. I actually try to get a picture in my head of what you're up to.

Paul And what do you see?

Susan Ah, ah, ah.

Paul Come on. What do you see?

Susan Well, darling . . .

Paul It's a pretty stupid thing to do, isn't it?

Susan Is it?

Paul I should say so. Pretty stupid pointless fucking thing to do. Lying on the bed in the middle of the afternoon. What the fuck are you doing lying on the bed in the afternoon? You shouldn't be lying on the bed in the afternoon. What's wrong with you? There's nothing wrong with you. If there's anything wrong with you we'll find you a better fucking hospital. A better fucking hospital and find some pills that really do the trick.

Susan Hey, hey, hey.

Paul But there's nothing wrong with you. There's nothing wrong. You think the world's such a bad place? You talk to Stephen and you think that the world is such a bad place, then fucking do something about it.

Susan (*going to door*)   Mina. Mina.

Paul Writing. Discussions. Just fucking do something. For the losers. Take them some clothes. Go through the wardrobe and take them some clothes. Or take them some food. Bake a fucking fruit cake. Bake a hundred fucking fruit cakes and go out to the villages and give out the fruit cake. And help instead of lying on the fucking bed in the afternoon.

Susan   Mina. I'm calling you.

Paul   I'm talking to you.

Susan   No you're not.

Paul   Why is your life so petty? Why is your existence so utterly meaningless?

Susan   I'll talk to Mina and we'll get the food on the table.

Paul   So meaningless that you have to imagine me at a desk in the afternoon.

Susan   Hold your horses. The food's on its way.

Paul   I don't want the fucking food.

Susan   Yes you do. Yes you do. Your blood sugar –

Paul   Fuck's sake.

Susan   – has now swung into the danger zone.

Paul   Blood sugar in the danger zone? Where do you get this, where does this – ?

Susan   You're always like this. The danger zone spells tetchiness.

Paul   What is this? Some clip you've seen?

Susan   We need to treat this as soon as we possibly can.

Paul   I'm not your patient. I'm not here for –

Susan   Let's feed you, darling. Let's feed you and everything will be alright.

Enter **Mina**.

Susan   Mina. Mina. Where is the food? The food is very late. We've been waiting. And it's not you that suffers. It's

never you that suffers. Mister is suffering because of his blood
sugar –

Paul   Agh.

Susan   And Miss is suffering because Mister is suffering and
Mister is now tetchy. Bread straight away. Supper as soon as
you can.

Exit **Mina**.

Susan   Like a child. Look at her. Never really understands.

Paul   Will we fuck tonight?

Susan   I don't know.

Paul   Really? Really? You don't know?

Susan   How should I know?

Paul   Maybe because . . .

Susan   It's not something we can plan for.

Paul   No.

Susan   I would really rather that was spontaneous.

Paul   Well, let's see, we haven't . . .

Susan   I'd rather that was something that just happened
between us.

Paul   It's been six months.

Susan   Has it?

Paul   Give or take – yes, six months.

Susan   Because, because . . .

Paul   So I should say . . . six months. At least. More like
seven or eight . . .

Susan   No.

Paul   Eight months. I should say the chances of a fuck
tonight are pretty slim.

Susan   Well maybe, yes, maybe.

Paul   I would say definitely.

Susan   Alright then.

Paul   I would say definitely zero.

Susan   Alright.

Paul   Why is that do you think?

Susan   Well, because . . .

Paul   Why is there nothing spontaneous happening between us?

Susan   I should say because . . . because . . .

Paul   Why do you sleep in Stephen's old room, wait till you think I'm asleep then pad along the corridor to Stephen's room?

Susan   Because . . .

Paul   Why have I been tossing myself to sleep for eight fucking months?

Susan   Because you always kept your eyes closed.

Paul   Did I?

Susan   Yes. Because your eyes were shut. Not just . . . squeezed tight. From start to finish.

Paul   Crap. Crap.

Susan   True. True. Fucking true and you know it. And you wept.

Paul   What?

Susan   Eyes squeezed tight with great tears down your cheeks.

Paul   This is . . .

Susan   Your chest holding in the . . . some grief. Grieving as we fucked.

Paul   No, no, no.

Susan   Please don't . . . Grieving as we fucked. And eventually . . . as a woman . . . you don't . . . you can't . . .

Paul   Why do you have to spout this shit? Why do you let this crap come out of your mouth?

Susan   I know. I saw.

Paul   Have you ever seen me cry? Do I look like a man who cries? Has there ever been a day . . . ? Christ, we've known each other for fucking generations. Under the last lot. Under the new lot. We've been together for so fucking long. And have I ever been a crying man?

Susan   Only when we –

Paul   So please don't give me this . . . because I really don't need this, this, this, this shit.

Susan   How can you just, just – ?

Paul   SHUT UP. SHUT THE FUCK UP.

Silence. Enter **Mina** *with bread on a plate.*

Susan   Thank you Mina. Did you get this from the – ? Well, you better get back to the . . . Mina, there's a chip on this plate. Do you know anything about this chip on the side of this plate here? Listen, you'd better get back to the supper.

Exit **Mina**.

Susan   Look at this. A chip on the side of the plate here. This was a new set this week. Pristine. She worked her way through the last lot. Boom. Crash. Clump. Sometimes I laugh at her. And sometimes I just block it all out. What can you do with a child? Here – it's good bread. I got it myself from the market. Mina never gets exactly what I want. So I've started to do the shopping myself. As of this month. And actually, you know, it's not such a hassle. Actually sometimes it can be quite good fun bargaining. I think I'll carry on. You need to eat.

Paul *takes a piece of bread and breaks bits off and eats them.*

Susan   It's amazing how quickly the blood sugar level goes back to normal. Just a bit of bread. One of those little miracles. Would you like to read Stephen's letter? He wrote to me. But I'm sure he wouldn't mind – I think he'd be happy if you read it.

Paul   I love you.

Susan   I put the letter down somewhere.

Paul   I love you.

Susan   I was reading it – I was here . . . and then I got distracted by Mina and I went to the . . . letter in my hand.

Paul   I love you.

Susan   And then I was on the bed in the dark.

Paul   I love you.

Susan   And then back in . . .

Paul   I love you.

Susan   So it must be – unless she's moved it of course, which is entirely possible . . .

Paul   I love you.

Susan   No. No. Here. Here.

Paul   What?

Susan   Stephen's letter. Do you want to read it?

Paul   Thank you.

He takes the letter.

He's always liked fruit cake.

Susan   Always.

Paul   Can you remember a time when he didn't like fruit cake?

Susan   No. No. I can't.

Paul   Maybe that's why he's always been so happy. Blood sugar's up, eh?

Susan   Yes, maybe that's it.

Paul   I think he's wasting his time.

Susan   Mmm?

Paul   Writing. Discussing. They never change anything.

Susan   Not immediately.

Paul   And then you . . . they actually want it, you know?

Susan   They?

Paul   They want to be Cut.

Susan   Hardly.

Paul   Oh yes, you listen to them. On the bus or . . . they actually want it.

Susan   They can't do.

Paul   You realise the tradition, the . . . it actually means something. It gives them meaning.

Susan   No. No.

Paul   That's the reality of the situation.

Susan   How do you know?

Paul   I overhear, I observe.

Susan   How can you say that?

Paul   Because I am actually out there, day after day. I actually –

Susan   And I'm . . . I go shopping. I go outside too.

Paul   Yes?

Susan   And I don't overhear . . . So you actually want this to go on? You don't want anything to change? You want this practice, this, well, frankly barbaric . . . you just want this to go on and on and on?

Paul   I'm tired.

Susan   Are you actually defending – ?

Paul   I'd love to talk to you. I'd love to debate with you. That would be a great pleasure. But actually after a day of work –

Susan   As I see it – Stephen says . . . you've actually got to be for it or against it.

Paul   Grow up.

Susan   That's what Stephen says.

Paul   Fuck's sake – Stephen is a child. Stephen is a student.

Susan   And I think I actually agree with him.

Paul   But you – you're a grown, you're a mature, you're an old, older woman, person, I think it's a bit late to be seeing the world in –

Susan   I think I may join a group.

Paul   – black and white. Goodies and baddies. Us and them. We Cut. They are Cut. Fucking simplistic fucking –

Susan   Or I may start, yes, actually I may start a group.

Paul   Life isn't simple. Things aren't simple. Don't simplify – let Stephen – fine, he's a student – maybe at the university but don't simplify –

Susan   You know what I saw this afternoon?

Paul   That's all I'm saying.

Susan   I lay on the bed this afternoon. In the dark. I took three pills. You're only supposed to take two but I felt . . .

I knew those plates were vulnerable and I was feeling . . .
anyway, I took three tablets and I lay back on the bed, I lay
back in the darkness and I tried to picture you . . .

Paul Listen . . .

Susan Which I've been doing quite a lot recently. The last
– oooh – six months. Lie on the bed in the afternoon and I
try to picture what you're doing at your office.

Paul Don't.

Susan And often I get no picture at all. Often, actually, my
mind's still here. And I'm anxious for the crockery and the
ornaments and the windows with Mina on the loose. No
pictures at all or sometimes a picture, very dull. You're filing.
Writing down some numbers. Few seconds of a very dull
picture. That's all it's been before.

Paul Yes.

Susan But today. But today. A very clear picture.
Suddenly. And you're Cutting. There's a young man. And
there's the instruments. And you're Cutting him.

Paul Yes.

Susan In your dull little office you were doing the Cut.
And I wonder why did that come into my head?

Paul Why do you think?

Susan I don't know. It was so clear.

Paul Were you awake?

Susan Oh yes. I was looking at the ceiling. Because I
noticed a mark. Maybe it was Stephen's letter? Do you think
that put the idea into my head?

Paul That's possible.

Susan That's the only thing that I can think of. Can you
think of anything else?

Paul The bread's all finished.

Susan   There's more. Mina will bring it.

Paul   I think I've had enough. I find sometimes . . . I get bloated.

Susan   You never said.

Paul   Oh yes. More than a couple of slices I find I have a tendency to get bloated.

Susan   You never told me that before.

Paul   It's a tiny, it's a small thing . . .

Susan   Maybe if we tried another . . .

Paul   It's only really started . . . in the last six months or so.

Susan   I see. I see. These things are sent to try us, aren't they?

Paul   I suppose that's right. Yes. These things are sent to try us. I thought of you this afternoon.

Susan   Really?

Paul   Physically. I thought about you physically this afternoon.

Susan   We'll try another kind of bread.

Paul   And I resolved . . . I'd like us to try again . . . physically. I'd like us to have another go.

Susan   Oh.

Paul   I'd like us to pick up where we left off. Lovemaking.

Susan   That's what you did in your office? Thought about us lovemaking?

Paul   Yes, yes, I did.

Susan   That was rather naughty.

Paul   Yes, yes, it was.

Susan   And I was here. Lying in the bed. Seeing you do the Cut.

Paul   Well.

Susan   Well.

Enter **Mina** *carrying a tray with two main courses and cutlery.*

Susan   Thank you, Mina. Better late than . . . there's a good girl. On the table.

Mina *lays the table.*

Susan   That's it, very good. Do you have a little girl or a little boy, Mina? Which is it? Boy or a girl? I tease her about it all day long. Don't I, Mina? Boy or girl, Mina? Boy or a girl? But she won't tell. You keep your secrets, don't you, Mina? You keep your cards close to your chest. But you've got a little kiddy tucked away at home. I know you do. I've got an instinct. There are no secrets from me, are there? I reckon a boy. We've got two boys. Do you want your boy to have the Cut, Mina? Like his ancestors. Course you don't. Makes you scared. Makes you angry. The Cut. Doesn't it, Mina? Well, don't you worry, Mina. Because that's all going to end. That's all going to change. My son's working on that. I'm working on that. We're going to get rid of the Cut. We're going to hunt them down and chuck them out. They'll be none of them left. There'll be none of them doing the Cut by the time your boy's a man. You'll see. You'll see. Yes. You've done very well. You've done beautifully. Oh, Mina – tomorrow, remind me when I go shopping – we're going to try a new type of bread. Mister is getting bloated so we're going to change the bread. Thank you. You go home. There's a kid waiting for you. Boy or girl, Mina? Boy or girl?

Exit **Mina**.

Susan *sits at the table.*

Susan   Well, this looks pretty good. Once she gets the job done, you know, she actually does it rather well. It's just getting her there that's the challenge. I bet you're hungry. Let's start, darling. Let's start.

Paul   I . . .

Susan   I chose all the ingredients myself.

Paul   I . . .

Susan   Bargained for every last bit of this.

Paul   I . . .

Susan   Meals have tasted better since I did the shopping.

Paul   I, I, I, I, I, I, I . . . (*Cries.*) . . . I, I, I, I, I, I, I . . . (*Cries.*)

Susan   You always feel better after you've eaten.

Paul   I, I, I, I, I, I, I . . . (*Cries/howls.*)

Susan   Darling. Darling. Darling.

Paul   A, a, a, a . . . (*Cries/howls.*)

Susan   You've never been the sort of man who cries. All the time I've known you. The last lot. The new lot. The generations. You've never been the sort that cries. How can I make love to you? How can I make love to a man who cries? Who shuts his eyes and just cries and cries.

Paul   I'm . . . sorry.

Susan   Well, of course you're sorry. We're all sorry. But we still have to eat.

Paul   I don't want this. I don't want . . .

Susan   Look at you. Look at you. Get up. You disgust me. You disgust me when you're like this.

Paul   Why can't I shoot myself?

Susan   That's a self-indulgence. There are children.

Paul   Why do we do this day after day after day?

Susan   I don't know. Because we have to. There are things in this world we just have to do. There are responsibilities.

Paul   Don't you ever cry?

Susan   No, no, no. Not that I remember. Not even this afternoon. Not even when I thought of you . . . no.

Paul   I'm sorry. Sorry. I won't do it again.

Susan   You won't . . . ?

Paul   There'll be no more tears.

Susan   Well, that's good. Shall we eat?

Paul   Yes. Let's eat.

They sit up at the table.

Susan   Tomorrow is fruit cake day. Baking for Stephen tomorrow. What will you be doing tomorrow.?

Paul   Same as always.

Susan   So I shall be very busy. No time for a lie-down tomorrow. No time to think about you.

Paul   That's good.

Susan   Yes, that's good. Isn't it? That's good.

Paul   I love you.

Susan   And then the next day we can drive to the university.

Paul   No. Please listen. Please listen to me. I love you. And I want . . . I wish I could show you all of myself. I wish I could let you into . . . I wish there was no . . .

Susan   Secrets?

Paul   Barriers. I wish there were no barriers.

Susan   Yes. Maybe that would be better.

Paul   But I can't.

Susan   No?

Paul   I want to protect you. I want to protect us. The comfort.

Susan   And is that working? Is . . . this . . . the answer?

Paul   I don't know. Will you stay in the bed with me – all night?

Susan   If that's what you'd like.

Paul   I'd like that very much.

Susan   Alright then. Alright. That's what we'll do.

Paul   I think if we just lie tighter for a night. If we could lie together in the dark and, and, and hold each other then that could be a start.

Susan   Do you have a greasy fork?

Paul   It's a very small thing but I think it would start to make it better.

Susan   Good.

Paul   There is a working party. I heard there was a working party looking into reform.

Susan   Mmm?

Paul   Of the Cut. Within government. There's talk of reform. That's where it will happen. Not with the . . . students. There's a movement within government.

Susan   Well . . . good.

Paul   I think the days are numbered.

Susan   Well don't tell me. Tell Stephen. He's the one to tell. I'm sure he'll be very interested. Will you talk to him on Saturday?

Paul   Of course.

Susan   Well . . . good.

Paul I'm a good man. At the end of the day I'm a good man.

Susan Of course you are. Is your fork clean?

Paul I think so.

Susan Then please . . . eat.

Scene Three

A room. **Paul** *and* **Stephen**.

Paul You still look the same.

Stephen Yes?

Paul To me. When I look at you, you still look the same. Six months. Sicking up milk on my shoulder. Three years running through the grass. Eighteen. Off to the university. You always looked exactly the same to me.

Stephen Right.

Paul And here you are. I look at you. And you still look . . . nothing's changed. To me. Nothing's changed.

Stephen Dad.

Paul But maybe you . . . what do you . . . how does it feel to you . . . ?

Stephen Yeah.

Paul Does it feel to you, does it feel to you that you've changed?

Stephen Yes.

Paul Ah.

Stephen Yes, it does.

Paul Ah.

Stephen I feel as though I've changed.

Paul　Ah.

Stephen　I feel as though, I feel . . . the world has changed. And I have changed.

Paul　Ah.

Stephen　I feel that very strongly.

Paul　Ah, ah, ah, ah. Youth. You're young.

Stephen　Not so –

Paul　But still young. Still young enough. Still young enough not to see . . .

Stephen　Yes?

Paul　It all comes round again. You do the same old stuff again and again and again.

Stephen　No.

Paul　Oh yes. There's only so much shit in the pot and it's swilling around and you're stuck in there long enough you'll spot the same old turds flying your way.

Stephen　No.

Paul　That's the way it is. You listen to me. I'm an old cunt. And old cunts . . . old cunts know this sort of thing.

Stephen　There's been a change.

Paul　Ha!

Stephen　There's been a change. Everything's been turned on its head.

Paul　Black is white. Good is bad.

Stephen　We're starting all over again. All of us together are starting together all over again.

Paul　Very good.

Stephen　There's a chance together to start to build –

Paul   Fantastic. Terrific. I'm proud of you. Good with words. You're good with words. You can outgibber the best. That's good. You were always like that. I can never quite . . . I always . . . suspected words. But you – straight into bed with the little fuckers and start banging away. That's good. Good. Good.

Stephen   This really is a better world.

Paul   You know they turn the light on at five thirty every morning? Every morning that fucking thing goes snap at half past five.

Stephen   I'll have a word.

Paul   Apart from Sundays when – oh, blessed luxury! – it's six o'clock. We're indulged till six on a Sunday.

Stephen   I'll talk to them. See if we can sort something out.

Paul   I don't want favours.

Stephen   I'm listened to.

Paul   I don't need you pulling any favours for me. Don't you do any fucking favours on my account. I'm my own person. You're your own person. You don't want to be accused of, of, of . . . favours.

Stephen   They're, we're not cruel.

Paul   They'll be watching out for that. You've always got to watch out for that. A new lot. Favours being pulled.

Stephen   So you don't want me to try . . . ?

Paul   I don't want you to try anything.

Stephen   Alright. Alright.

Paul   What I want, what I want, what I want, what I want is for you to, to leave well alone.

Stephen   Alright then.

Paul   Just . . . let it be.

Stephen   Okay.

Paul   How's your mother?

Stephen   She's fine.

Paul   Good. Good. Good.

Stephen   Mina lost her baby.

Paul   The light goes off soon.

Stephen   Mina had a baby. Inside her. Mina was pregnant. But then she lost the baby. Mother helped with the funeral. She dug.

Paul   Your mother?

Stephen   Yes. She dug the hole.

Paul   Your mother dug the hole? Your mother dug a hole? Oh. Ha, ha, ha! I'm sorry. But that is fucking funny. Don't you think that is fucking funny?

Stephen   I . . .

Paul   No. I'm sorry. Come on. The thought of your mother, the thought of your mother, the thought of her actually standing there with a spade and the earth and the . . . that is fucking funny, isn't it?

Stephen   Is it?

Paul   Well, of course it is. Of course it is. What's . . . can't you see the humour in . . . ?

Stephen   No.

Paul   Oh come on. Have you lost all . . . ? Laugh, for fuck's sake. Smile. Just let yourself . . . Fuck. Fuck. Fuck.

Stephen   Everything's changed. Everything's new. And in the new circumstances . . .

Paul   Yes? Yes?

Stephen   And in the new circumstance it is quite appropriate, it is fitting, it is right, that my mother, that your wife, should dig a hole.

Paul   Listen to yourself. Listen to yourself.

Stephen   Dad.

Paul   Dig a hole? You sound comical. You sound . . . ridiculous. You sound fucking ridiculous.

Stephen   To you maybe.

Paul   So get down off your high . . . stop being so fucking pompous. And laugh.

Stephen   That's not appropriate.

Paul   At yourself. At her. At me. If you like – come on. Rip the piss out of me. Rip the piss out of this whole shitty shebang.

Stephen   I don't want to.

Paul   Christ's sake, fuck's sake . . . is there no humanity left? Do you none of you have a little fucking speck of humanity?

Stephen   Don't you tell me – don't you tell me –

Paul   Alright.

Stephen   – about humanity. How can you tell me about humanity when you, you . . . ?

Paul   Alright, alright, alright.

Stephen   When you . . . the Cut. It's not me, it's not us . . . we never . . . year after year . . . the instruments . . .

Paul   Yes.

Stephen   Humanity? Humanity? Humanity?

Paul   You're right. Did you never think . . . ?

Stephen   No.

Paul   All the years and you never thought for a . . . ?

Stephen   No.

Paul   I was a good dad.

Stephen   Yes.

Paul   I think your mother always knew.

Stephen   She says not.

Paul   Every day a little dance around each other because I suspected that she suspected.

Stephen   She told the tribunal –

Paul   Sometimes it was actually quite fun.

Stephen   She told the tribunal that there was never the faintest inkling.

Paul   Did she?

Stephen   Yes.

Paul   Did she really?

Stephen   Yes.

Paul   Well, well, well. Well, I suppose she would. Each to their own, I suppose. You've got to save your own bacon when the chips are down, isn't that right?

Stephen   I think she's telling the truth.

Paul   Oh no, no, no.

Stephen   I could see it in her eyes.

Paul   No, no, no, because I spent the years, I had the years with . . . so don't you . . . no. Lying.

Stephen   No.

Paul   So – this is the bright new future. This is the new world. Kids who can't tell the difference between a lie and the truth. Oh son. Oh son, I would weep but there's no more fucking tears.

Stephen   The tribunal cleared Mother.

Paul   Well, that's good.

Stephen   But the house was in your name, so . . .

Paul   Ah . . .

Stephen   They're using it as a prison.

Paul   More prisons? A better world with more prisons?

Stephen   There are certain temporary . . .

Paul   Yes, of course. Of course. Of course. Would you say I'm evil?

Stephen   I . . .

Paul   No. Just look at me now. And would you say I'm evil?

Stephen   I . . .

Paul   No. The heart. The gut. The soul. Listen. Listen. Listen to them now. And would you say . . .

Stephen   Yes.

Paul   . . . that I'm evil?

Stephen   Yes.

Paul   Ah.

Stephen   Yes. There are systems of evil. There are acts of evil. There are people of evil. I say that there are all of these things. Yes. There is evil. And you are evil. You are it. You are my father and you are evil. That's what I say. Yes. Yes. Yes.

Paul   I see.

Stephen   That's not personal . . . please don't take that the wrong . . .

Paul   It's alright.

Stephen   Please. I'm sorry. I'm sorry.

Paul   No. Don't be. I bless you. Come here. Let me hold you.

Stephen   No.

Paul   Please. Let me hold you so I can bless you for that.

Stephen *moves to* **Paul**. **Paul** *holds him.*

Paul   Bless you for that. Bless you for that. Bless you for that.

Stephen *moves away.*

Paul   You're honest. I'll give you that. We were never honest. Me. Your mother. The whole lot of us. We were never honest but you're . . .

Stephen   I try.

Paul   So maybe it's better, yes? Maybe that's a bit better than before?

Stephen   We like to think so.

Paul   Cold but honest. You are the future, my son.

Stephen   And you . . .

Paul   And I'm . . . yeah, well, you're right about me. What you say. I'm . . . yes, I am. Totally. In act and, and, and, and . . . soul. Totally.

Stephen   But if you just . . .

Paul   No.

Stephen   There is forgiveness. That's what we . . .

Paul   No.

Stephen   The Ministry of Forgiveness has hearings. You'll be heard. I can arrange for you to be heard. If you say what you've just said to me, you acknowledge, you can . . .

Paul   No.

Stephen   There is a way forward.

Paul   I don't want to . . . no. I want punishment.

Stephen   There are no −

Paul   I want to be paraded and scourged and feel the blood in my eyes and see the blades before me. I want to know that everyone sees my rottenness and is ready to Cut it out.

Stephen   What? What?

Paul   I am the dirt that needs to be destroyed so you can be purified.

Stephen   What? Where do you get the . . . ? No. No.

Paul   That's what I want.

Stephen   That's so . . . old-fashioned.

Paul   Yes. Isn't it? Isn't it? Isn't it?

Stephen   That doesn't happen any more.

Paul   I know. I know. So. I'll sit it out. Lights on at five-thirty, six days a week. Sunday indulgence. Sit it out till there's a new lot or this lot falls back on some of the old ways.

Stephen   That isn't going to happen.

Paul   It always happens. Sooner or later. Sooner or later when the forgiveness is done there'll be scourging again and I'll be here. I'll be ready for it. It's what I deserve. I'm evil. It's what I deserve. The light's going to go. Any moment now that light's going to go blink and then there's going to be total blackness. So you had better piss off. Go on. Go on.

Stephen   Dad.

Paul   You don't want to get stuck in the darkness. You go. There's a better world out there.

Stephen   Goodbye.

Citizenship

Citizenship was developed by the NT Shell Connections 2005 programme and premiered in the Cottesloe auditorium of the National Theatre, London, in March 2006. The cast was as follows:

Amy	Claire-Louise Cordwell
Tom	Sid Mitchell
Gary	Matt Smith
Ray	Robert Boulter
Stephen	Andrew Garfield
Kerry	Farzana Dua Elahe
Chantel	Andrea Riseborough
Alicia	Naomi Bentley
De Clerk	Richard Dempsey
Melissa	Matti Houghton
Tarot Reader	Joy Richardson
Baby	Alex Tregear
Martin	Javone Prince
Directed by	Anna Mackmin
Designed by	Jonathan Fensom
Lighting by	Jason Taylor
Music by	Paddy Cunneen
Sound Designer	Christopher Shutt

One

Amy, **Tom**.

Amy   You got the Nurofen?

Tom   Yeah.

Amy   Take four.

Tom   It says two.

Amy   Yeah, but if you're gonna really numb yourself you gotta do four.

Tom   I dunno.

Amy   Do you want it to hurt?

Tom   No.

Amy   Then take four. Here.

Amy *passes* **Tom** *vodka. He uses it to wash down four Nurofen.*

Amy   Now put the ice cube on your ear.

Tom *does this.*

Amy   Now you gotta hold it there till you can't feel nothing.

Tom   Thanks for helping

Amy   It's gonna look good.

Tom   Yeah?

Amy   Yeah, really suit you.

Tom   Thass good.

Amy   You got a nice face.

Tom   I don't like my face.

Amy   I think it's nice.

Tom   Sometimes I look in the mirror and I wish I was dead.

Amy   I got rid of mirrors.

Tom   Yeah.

Amy   Mum read this feng shui thing and it said I wasn't supposed to have them. You numb now?

Tom   Almost. You got a nice face.

Amy   You don't have to lie.

Tom   I'm not. You're fit.

Amy   I know I'm plain. But that's okay. I talked to my therapist.

Tom   What did she say?

Amy   That I have to love myself in case nobody else does.

Tom   Your mum loves you.

Amy   I suppose. You ready now?

Tom   I reckon.

Amy *produces a needle.*

Tom   Is that clean?

Amy   I put it in Dettol.

Tom   Alright.

Amy   Let's start.

She starts to push the needle into **Tom***'s ear but he pulls away.*

Amy   I can't do it if you do that.

Tom   I know.

Amy   You gotta sit still.

Tom   Maybe we should leave it. Maybe not today.

Amy   I thought you wanted an earring.

Tom   I know.

Amy   Thass what you been saying for weeks: I wanna earring, I wanna earring.

Tom   I know, only –

Amy   I'll go careful. Come here. You're a baby.

Tom   No.

Amy   I'll treat you nice and soft. Like a baby.

Tom   Alright.

He comes back.

Amy   Bit more vodka.

Tom *drinks.*

Amy   Bit more.

Tom *drinks.*

Amy   Bit more.

Tom *drinks.* **Amy** *pushes the needle into his ear.*

Tom   Aaaagggghhh.

Amy   Thass it.

Tom   It hurts.

Amy   Nearly there.

Tom   Do it quickly. Do it. Aggghhh.

Amy   Soon be finished.

Tom   Right. Right. Is there blood?

Amy   What?

Tom   Is there blood?

Amy   I dunno.

Tom   I can feel blood

Amy   Maybe a bit.

Tom   Shit. Shit. Shit.

Amy   It's not much. You're gonna be alright.

Tom   Yeah. Yeah. Yeah. Yeah. Yeah. Yeah. Yeah.

He faints.

Amy   Tom? Tom! Shit. Shit.

She drinks a lot of vodka.

Tom – please.

Her mobile rings.

(*On phone.*) Kez? No. I'm fucking – I'm having a panic attack. Like I used to, yeah. Tom's dead. He's died. Just now. Shit. I killed him. I've killed Tom. I wanna kill myself. Shit.

Tom *groans.*

Amy (*on phone*)   He made a noise. Yeah, well. He came back to life. I gotta go. Kez – I'm going now.

Tom   Whass going on?

Amy   You sort of went.

Tom   Who's on the phone?

Amy   Thass Kerry. She's getting stressed out cos she's gotta give the baby back tomorrow.

Tom   Baby?

Amy   Life Skills.

Tom   Oh yeah.

Amy   You remember Life Skills? Each of the girls has gotta take it in turns to looks after this baby – plastic baby. It puts you off having a real one. You could have memory loss.

Tom   No.

Amy   Like Shareen after the overdose. Her mum and dad went to see her in the hospital and she didn't know who they were.

Tom   I haven't got memory loss.

Amy   Alright.

Tom   Fucking stupid idea letting you do that. I should have gone to a fucking professional. Fucking go to somebody who knows what they're fucking doing 'stead of letting you fucking fuck the whole thing up.

Amy   I was trying to help.

Tom   Yeah, well, you're no help – you're rubbish. You're total rubbish.

Amy   Don't give me negative messages.

Tom   Trying to kill me with your stupid needle.

Amy   I can't be around people who give me negative messages.

Tom   I fucking hate you.

Amy   No. I'm sorry. I'm sorry. I'm sorry.

She cries.

Tom   Come on. Don't. No. No.

Amy   I can't do anything right. I'm useless.

Tom   No.

Amy   I am. Thass why I cut myself. Cos I'm totally useless. Ughhh.

Tom   Hey hey hey.

He holds **Amy**.

Tom   Come on. Alright. Alright. Alright. You better?

Amy   I dunno.

Tom   You're alright. You're a good person. I like you.

Amy   Yeah?

Tom   I really like you.

Amy   Thass good.

Tom   You got a nice face.

Amy *kisses* **Tom.**

Tom   Oh.

Amy   Was that wrong?

Tom   I didn't mean you to do that.

Amy   Oh. Right. Right.

Tom   I didn't wanna kiss you. Only –

Amy   Yeah?

Tom   I'm not ready for . . .

Amy   You're fifteen.

Tom   I know.

Amy   You gotta have done . . .

Tom   No.

Amy   Why?

Tom   It doesn't matter.

Amy   Tell me.

Tom   I have this dream. And in this dream I'm kissing someone. Real kissing. Tongues and that. But I can't see who I'm kissing. I don't know if it's a woman. Or a man. I try to see the face. But I can't.

Amy   Are you gay?

Tom   I don't know.

Amy   There's bisexuals.

Tom   You won't tell anyone?

Amy   No. Are you going to decide?

Tom   What?

Amy   What you are?

Tom   I don't know.

Amy   Or find out?

Tom   I don't know.

Amy   Don't waste yourself, Tom. You've got a nice face.

Tom   Yeah.

Amy *gets a text message.*

Amy   It's Kerry. She says the baby's gone to sleep.

Tom   It's not real.

Amy   It is to her.

Tom   I'm gonna go.

Amy   Finish off the vodka.

Tom   No. Thanks. Forget what I told you.

Amy   You're still bleeding. There's still some –

Tom   I got coursework.

Exit **Tom***.* **Amy** *drinks.*

Two

Gary, **Tom***. They are smoking a joint.*

Tom   Good draw.

Gary   Got it off my mum's boyfriend for my birthday.
Ten big fat ones for my fifteenth.

Tom   Thass cool.

Gary   Thass the last. He had a fight with his dealer last night. Dealer come round the house and they had a big barney. An' me mum's ragga CDs got smashed in the ruck.

Tom   Shit.

Gary   Yeah. She is well gutted.

Enter **Ray** *and* **Stephen**.

Ray   Wass 'appening?

Gary   Chilling.

Ray   You shag Amy last night? We wanna know. You get jiggy?

Stephen   Jiggy-jiggy.

Ray   Is she your bitch? You ride her like your bitch?

Tom   Fuck's sake.

Gary   You got problems.

Ray   What?

Gary   I'm saying: you got problems.

Ray   What you saying? I got problems.

Gary   Yeah, you got problems. No respec'.

Ray   I respec'.

Gary   No respec' for woman.

Ray   I respec' woman.

Gary   Ride her like a bitch? Didn't he say?

Tom   Yeah.

Ray   That's what I said.

Stephen   He said it.

Ray   That's what I said. I ride her *and* respec' woman.

Stephen   Yeah. Ride and respec'.

Ray   You chat shit. What are you? What is he?

Stephen   He is gay.

Gary   All I'm saying –

Ray   So gay. You are so totally gay, Gary.

Gary   Just sayin' –

Ray   You are like the most totally gay person anyone knows.

Gary   I'm not.

Ray   Gay Gary. Thass what you are. Respec'? What are you chattin'? You're chattin' gay. You are fucking wrong, man. Wrong in your head. Wrong in your, your . . . hormones, man. Totally totally wrong.

Gary   Thass not right.

Ray (*to* **Tom**)   Come on, man. Say something. Tell him.

Tom   I . . .

Ray   You're always watching. You're never talking. Tell him.

Tom   Listen, I wanna –

Ray   You fucking tell him.

Stephen   Tell the battyboy.

Ray   You fucking tell him.

Tom   . . . You're gay, Gary.

Gary   Shit.

Tom   Everyone says it. Everyone call you it. Gay Gary.

Gary   I know what they say.

Tom   You shouldn't talk gay.

Stephen   Thass right.

Tom   Cos no one likes a person who talks gay.

Gary   You chat shit, Tom.

Ray   Listen, he's tellin' you –

Gary   Same as them. All of you. Chattin' shit. All day long. Mouths moving but it's just: chat, chat, chat. Shit, shit, shit.

Tom   No, no.

Gary   Yeah, yeah.

Tom   No.

Gary   Yeah.

Ray   Fight fight fight.

Stephen   Fight fight fight.

Ray   Fight fight fight.

Stephen   Fight.

Tom *pushes* **Gary**.

Ray   Thass it.

Stephen   Do it back or you're gay.

Gary   Fuck's sake.

Gary *pushes* **Tom.**

Ray   Fucking insulted you, man. The gay boy insulted you.

Stephen   Batty hit yer.

Ray   Get him.

Tom   Listen –

Ray   Use your fist.

Stephen   Fist for the battyboy.

Gary   Go on.

Tom   Yeah?

Gary   Do what they tell you. Do what they want to.

Tom   Yeah?

Gary   Follow the leader.

Tom   Yeah.

Tom *punches* **Gary** *in the stomach.*

Ray   Respec', man.

Stephen   Total respec'.

Gary   Fuck you.

Gary *punches* **Tom** *in the stomach very hard.* **Tom** *falls over.*

Ray   Nasty.

Enter **Amy, Kerry, Alicia, Chantal. Chantal** *carries the baby.*

Kerry   You're not carrying her properly.

Chantal   Leave it, Kez.

Kerry   But you're not doing the head right.

Chantal   It's my baby, Kez.

Kerry   I know.

Chantal   Yesterday it was yours and now it's mine.

Kerry   I'm only telling you.

Chantal   An' I can do whatever I want with it.

Amy   She's got withdrawal symptoms.

Chantal   Over plastic?

Kerry   Don't say that. You're not fit.

Alicia   Iss the Blazin' Squad. You mellowin'?

Ray   Totally chilled, me darlin'.

Stephen   Totally.

Alicia   Sweet.

Ray   Hear Tom was round yours last night.

Amy   Thass right.

Ray   Gettin' jiggy.

Amy   Do what?

Ray   Jiggy-jiggy-jiggy.

Stephen   Jiggy-jiggy-jiggy.

Amy   You say that?

Tom   No.

Ray   What? You never?

Amy   Thass right.

Ray   What? He not fit enough for you?

Amy   Iss not that.

Ray   You frigid? She frigid, Tom?

Tom   No.

Ray   Wass wrong with 'em? Why ain't they gettin' jiggy?

Alicia   I dunno.

Ray   Thass gay.

Tom   What?

Ray   Youse two are so gay.

Tom/Amy   No.

Ray   Oooo – sore.

Amy   Your ear's started.

Tom   Yeah?

Amy   You started bleeding again.

Alicia   Shit. There's blood.

Kerry   I don't wanna look.

Amy   You wanna look after that. You got a hanky?

Tom   No.

Amy   Chantal?

Chantal   Here.

Chantal *tucks the baby under her arm to find a paper hanky.*

Kerry   You can't do that.

Chantal   Juss for a moment.

Kerry   You got to hold it properly all day long.

Chantal   Juss while I'm lookin'.

Kerry   Give it me. Give it me.

Kerry *takes the baby from* **Chantal**. **Chantal** *finds the hanky, passes it to* **Amy**. **Amy** *holds the hanky on* **Tom**'s *ear.*

Kerry (*to baby*)   Alright. Alright.

Amy   You wanna hold that there?

Ray   She bite you?

Stephen   Yeah.

Ray   While you were doing it?

Tom   It'll be alright now.

Amy   You sure?

Tom   Yeah.

Tom *continues to hold the handkerchief on his ear.*

Chantal   Give me the baby, Kerry.

Kerry   Later.

Chantal   Now.

Kerry   Bit longer.

Chantal   I gotta have it for Life Skills.

Kerry   I know.

Chantal   So . . . ?

Alicia   Give it, Kez.

Kerry   Juss . . . do the head properly.

Chantal   Alright.

Kerry *hands* **Chantal** *the baby.*

Alicia   Thass it. Come on.

Exit **Alicia**, **Kerry**, **Chantal**.

Amy   Laters.

Exit **Amy**.

Ray   How do you do the ear? She do that ear? Was she like eatin' you?

Tom   Won't stop bleeding.

Ray   What do you do?

Tom   It was . . . we were doing an earring?

Ray   Earring? Earring? Earring? Shit man. In that ear? You was doing an earring in that ear? Shit, man. Thass the gay side. Shit. You was doing an earring in the gay side. Shit.

Stephen   Shit.

Tom   No. No. I'm jokin'. It was –

Ray   Yeah? Yeah?

Tom   It wasn't –

Ray   Yeah? Yeah?

Tom   It was bitin'.

Ray   Yeah?

Stephen   Yeah?

Tom   It was like love-biting.

Ray   I knew it.

Stephen   Thass right.

Tom   We were gettin' hot and biting and that and we −

Ray   Yeah?

Tom   And we got −

Stephen   Jiggy.

Tom   Yeah. Jiggy.

Ray   I knew it.

Tom   Yeah, totally jiggy. Like ridin' and ridin' and ridin'.

Ray   Oh yeah.

Tom   And she was wantin' it.

Stephen   Yeah.

Tom   And I was givin' like, like, like, like −

Ray   Yeah.

Tom   A big man.

Ray   Thass right. Big man.

Stephen   Big man.

Ray   Big man.

Stephen   Big man.

Ray   Big man.

Stephen   Big man.

Gary   Hey − that's sweet.

Ray   Shut it, gay boy.

Stephen   The big man is talkin', battyboy.

Ray   Out of ten?

Tom   She's a six.

Ray   So you see her again?

Tom   Maybe. I'm thinkin' about it.

Stephen   De Clerk.

Ray   Run.

Gary   Give us a hand.

Ray   On your own, man.

Ray *and* **Stephen** *exit rapidly.* **Tom** *goes to help* **Gary**. *Enter* **De Clerk**.

De Clerk   Tom.

Tom   Sir?

De Clerk   A word – now. Gary – move.

Gary   Sir.

De Clerk   You're a stoner, Gary.

Gary   The herb is the people's weed.

De Clerk   Piss off.

Exit **Gary**. **De Clerk** *pulls out a piece of coursework.*

De Clerk   What's this, Tom?

Tom   My Citizenship, sir.

De Clerk   Your Citizenship coursework. And what's this?

Tom   Blood, sir.

De Clerk   Blood on your Citizenship coursework. Blood on the work which tomorrow inspectors are going to want to see.

Tom   I know, sir.

De Clerk   And it's not going to be you that's going to be bollocked, is it? No. It's going to be me. Didn't I say, didn't I say many, many – oh so many – times that your coursework should be neat?

Tom   Yes, sir.

De Clerk   Because I don't need the hassle from the inspectors. Because I'm very stressed out. I'm not sleeping. I told you all that I wasn't sleeping. Some nights nothing. Some nights just a couple of hours.

Tom   I know, sir.

De Clerk   The Head gives me grief, kids give me grief. And now tomorrow the inspection team arrives and what do I find?

Tom   I'm sorry, sir.

De Clerk   I find that you have been bleeding all over 'What Does a Multicultural Society Mean to Me?'.

Tom   I didn't mean to.

De Clerk   I'm not showing this to the inspectors. You can stay behind tonight and copy this out.

Tom   But sir –

De Clerk   You want me to copy it out? I've got lesson plans, marking. I'm going to be here till midnight. I'm not copying it out. You'll see me at the end of school and you'll copy this out.

Tom   Yes, sir.

De Clerk   Right then. See you tonight.

Exit **De Clerk**. **Tom** *mops his ear. The bleeding has stopped. Enter* **Amy**.

Amy   Why you tell 'em you slept with me?

Tom   I never.

Amy   Don't lie. You tole Ray and Steve. Now they tole everyone.

Tom   I'm sorry.

Amy   But it's not true.

Tom   I know.

Amy   So why you – ? You gotta sort out what you are, Tom. You straight? You gay?

Tom   Don't say it in school.

Amy   You bisexual? If you want you can see my therapist. My mum'll sort it out.

Tom   I don't need a therapist.

Amy   I know somewhere they do tarot. The card might tell you.

Tom   I don't believe in that.

Amy   What you gonna do, Tom? You gotta stop lying. You gotta decide what you are.

Tom   I know.

Three

Tom and **De Clerk**. **Tom** *holds a bloody handkerchief to his ear.*

Tom   I'm still bleeding, sir.

De Clerk   Just – copy it out.

Tom   I am. I'm just . . . worried.

De Clerk   Mmmmmm.

Tom   You know – worried that I might copy it but then I might drip blood on the, like, copy, you know.

De Clerk   Well, don't.

Tom   I'm trying, only –

De Clerk   Put the paper over there, lean your head over there.

Tom   Alright. (*Does this*.) It feels really weird, sir.

De Clerk   Shut up.

Tom   I'm not writing straight, sir.

De Clerk   Do the best you can.

Tom   I'm trying hard but it's not going straight, sir.

De Clerk   Fuck's sake, Tom.

Tom   Thought so. I just dripped. Blood on the folder.

De Clerk   Haven't you got a plaster?

Tom   I asked at the front office, but the rules say we have to provide our own.

De Clerk   Well, alright – just try not to drip any more.

Tom   Doing my best.

De Clerk's *mobile rings.*

Tom   You gonna get that, sir?

De Clerk   No.

Mobile stops.

Tom   Might have been important.

De Clerk   Nothing else matters. Nothing else matters but your coursework and the inspectors and that we don't become a failing school, okay? There is nothing else in the whole wide world that matters apart from that.

Mobile rings again.

Tom   They don't think so.

De Clerk   Well fuck 'em, fuck 'em, fuck 'em.

Tom   They really want to talk to you.

De Clerk   Uhhh.

He answers the mobile.

No. Still at − I told you. I told you. Because we've got the inspectors. No. No. Well, put it in the fridge and I'll . . . put it in the bin. I don't care. I don't care. I can't.

He ends the call.

Tom   Are you married, sir?

De Clerk   I'm not talking any more.

Tom   I was just wondering.

De Clerk   Well, don't.

Tom   Other teachers say: my wife this or my girlfriend that. But you never do.

De Clerk   Well, that's up to them.

Tom   It makes you wonder. We all wonder.

De Clerk   Listen, I'm here from eight in the morning until eight in the evening, midnight the last few weeks − maybe I don't have a personal life.

Tom   Yeah.

De Clerk   Maybe I'm not a person at all. Maybe I'm just lesson plans and marking.

Tom   Yeah. Maybe.

De Clerk   Oh. My head. Have you got a Nurofen?

Tom   Sorry, sir?

De Clerk   Have you got a Nurofen or something?

Tom   No, sir. I had some but I took them all.

De Clerk   Right.

Tom   If you want to go home – go home to your . . . partner.

De Clerk   I can't.

Tom   I can do a massage, sir. I know how to do a massage.

De Clerk   No.

Tom   It stops headaches. I done it loads of times.

De Clerk   Listen. Physical contact is –

Tom   Out of lessons now.

De Clerk   Difficult.

Tom   Shhhhhh. Our secret.

He moves over to **De Clerk** *and massages his shoulders and neck.*

Tom   You've got to breathe too. Remember to keep breathing.

De Clerk   Mmmmm.

Tom   There's a lot of stress about, isn't there?

De Clerk   It's all stress.

Tom   How old are you?

De Clerk   Twenty-two.

Tom   Lots of teachers burn out before they're twenty-five because of all the stress.

De Clerk   Mmmmm.

Tom   You're quite developed, sir. Do you go to the gym?

De Clerk   Sometimes.

Tom   With your . . . partner.

De Clerk   Back to your work now. That was wrong. Physical contact.

Tom Sir – I'm really sorry, but I've –

Tom *wipes* **De Clerk**'s *shoulder.*

Tom I've dripped on you, sir.

De Clerk What?

Tom You've got blood on your shirt.

De Clerk Oh fuck.

Tom I'm really sorry. It's a really nice shirt.

De Clerk Shit. Shit. Shit.

He scrubs at his shoulder.

Tom If you want me to get you another one, sir –

De Clerk No no.

Tom I get a discount. My brother manages Top Man.

De Clerk Tom – get on with your work. You get on with your work and I'll get on with my work.

Tom You've got good clothes, sir. For a teacher.

De Clerk Tom.

Pause.

Tom Sir . . . I keep on having this dream and in this dream I'm being kissed.

De Clerk Don't.

Tom Only I never know whether it's a man or woman who's doing the kissing.

De Clerk This isn't Biology. I'm Citizenship.

Tom I think I dream about being kissed by a man.

De Clerk I don't want to know about that.

Tom I really want to know: so I dream about a man kissing me?

De Clerk   Please. Don't do this. I'm tired. I'm exhausted. I've got the Head of Department chasing me. I've got the inspectors coming after me like wolves after blood. I've still got eight hours of paperwork. And I've done a full day's teaching. Please understand the pressure I'm under and just copy the work.

Tom   What do you do if you're gay, sir?

De Clerk   You talk to someone.

Tom   I'm trying to talk to you.

De Clerk   You don't talk to me. Talk to your form tutor.

Tom   He hates me.

De Clerk   I don't think so.

Tom   What do you do at the weekends, sir?

De Clerk   Alright. Go away. Go home.

Tom   What about the coursework?

De Clerk   I'll explain the blood to the inspectors.

Tom   Alright then.

He packs up his bag.

Bye then, sir.

De Clerk   Bye, Tom.

Tom   I want to talk to someone gay, sir. I don't know any.

De Clerk   Shut up, please shut up.

Tom   I really want to meet someone gay and ask them what it's like.

De Clerk   Well – it's fine. It's normal. It's just fine.

Tom   You reckon?

De Clerk   You know the school policy: we celebrate difference. You report bullies. Everything's okay. You're okay.

Tom   I don't feel okay.

De Clerk   Well – you should do.

Four

Gary, **Tom**. *Smoking a joint.*

Gary   Was it good?

Tom   What?

Gary   You know – when you done Amy?

Tom   Well . . .

Gary   Cos lovin'. There's so many types of lovin'.

Tom   Yeah?

Gary   Yeah. Between man and woman. There's so many types of lovin', in't there?

Tom   You reckon?

Gary   Oh yeah. There's sweet lovin' and there's animal lovin' and there's hard lovin' and there's dirty lovin'. There's millions of ways of lovin'. You follow?

Tom   I think so.

Gary   You lie.

Tom   No.

Gary   I'm chattin' shit, aren't I?

Tom   No.

Gary   Yeah, I'm chattin' shit. Thass the herb. I always chat shit when I'm blazin'. But thass the way I like it. I like to chat shit.

Tom   I like the way you talk.

Gary   Yeah?

Tom   You talk good. You're better than the knobheads. Ray, Steve – they're knobheads.

Gary   Then how come you –

Tom   Yeah yeah.

Gary   – hit me when they tell you?

Tom   I'm sorry.

Gary   No worries. Love and understanding. Peace to you, brother.

Tom   Yeah, peace.

Gary   To mellow, man. Love you, brother.

Tom   Yeah. Brother love.

Gary *puts his arm round* **Tom***.*

Gary   You like the brother love?

Tom   Yeah, it's good.

Gary   Peace on the planet. No war. Herb bring harmony. Blaze some more?

Tom   Yeah.

Gary *produces another rolled joint from a tin.*

Gary   So tell me 'bout your lovin'?

Tom   Well –

Gary   Is she your woman now?

Tom   Well –

Gary   Or was it like a one-night lovin' ting?

Tom   Well –

Gary   Don't be shy. Take a big draw and tell.

He hands **Tom** *the joint.* **Tom** *draws.*

Gary   Harder, man. Draw as deep as you can.

Tom *draws as hard as he can.*

Tom   I need some water.

Gary   No. Not till you tell. Tell me what it was like. Come on, man.

Tom   I feel ill.

Gary   I gotta know. I gotta know about the ride.

Gary *pins* **Tom** *to the floor, knees over his arms, sitting on his chest.*

Gary   What was it like when you rode the woman?

Tom   Get off me – off me.

Gary   Jiggy-jiggy with the honey. Ya!

Tom   Off.

He pushes **Gary** *off.*

Tom   I never, alright? I never –

Gary   What?

Tom   I never done her. We never done anything.

Gary   What? Nothing? Oral? Finger?

Tom   Nothing, okay. We never done it.

Gary   Shit. You lied.

Tom   Yeah.

Gary   That's sad, man.

Tom   Yeah, it's really sad.

Gary   So – you not gonna tell me 'bout no lovin'?

Tom   No.

Gary   Shit, broth'. That was gonna be my wank tonight.

Tom   Yeah?

Gary   Yeah – your booty grindin' her. That was gonna –

Tom   Well, there's nothing.

Gary   You wanna pretend for me? Like make it up. So – you never done it. But you can make up like a story, like a dirty story so I got summat in my head.

Tom   I'm not good at stories.

Gary   Just make it dirty so I got something for tonight.

Tom   I'm still supposed to copy out my Citizenship for De Clerk.

Gary   Okay – tell me about your dreams. You gotta have dirty dreams.

Tom   Course.

Gary   Then tell me –

Tom   I don't know.

Gary   Come, brother love. (*Sits* **Tom** *down, puts his arms around him.*) Tell your brother.

Tom   . . . I have this dream. And in this dream I'm lying in bed. Not in my room. Not like my room at home. Like a strange room.

Gary   Like a dungeon?

Tom   No, maybe like a Travel Lodge or something, I don't know.

Gary   Right.

Tom   And I'm almost asleep but then the door opens and this stranger comes into the room.

Gary   Like a thief?

Tom   Maybe but this . . . person, they come over to the bed and they kiss me.

Gary   Right. And – ?

Tom   It's a person but I don't know, I don't know –

Gary   Yeah.

Tom   See, this person, are they a woman or are they . . . ?

Gary   Yeah?

Tom *leans over and kisses* **Gary** *on the lips.*

Gary   You're battyman?

Tom   I don't know.

Gary   Shit, blud, you're battyman. The battyman kissed me. Shit.

Gary *moves away and takes several draws.*

Tom   I don't know. Don't know. Just wanted to see, you know – just wanted to see what it felt like if I –

Gary   And did you like it?

Tom   I don't know.

Gary   Was my lips sweet?

Tom   I don't know.

Gary   No, blud, thass cool, thass cool, I can handle that. Peace to all. Everybody's different. I can go with that.

Tom   I'm sorry.

Gary   Hey – love you still, bro'.

He hugs **Tom**.

Tom   I just thought – you're Gay Gary.

Gary   Thass just a name. You touch my arse I kill you, see?

Tom   Okay.

Gary No, see, I like the honeys. You should see my site. Thass where I live out what's in my head, see?

He gets out his laptop, opens his website.

See, these are my fantasies. And I share him with the world on my message board. I got graphics, see?

Tom Is that you?

Gary Yeah.

Tom You got muscles.

Gary Yeah, well – thass me older, see. And thass my dick.

Tom (*laughs*) I thought it was a weapon.

Gary (*laughs*) Yeah. My dick's a lethal weapon. And I fight my way through the desert, see, through all the terrorists and that, see? Nuke nuke nuke. And then when I get to the city – there's all the honeys, see? And I ride 'em, see. And then I kill 'em.

Tom That's sick, man. I thought you was all love and understanding.

Gary Can't help what's in my head. Gotta let it out.

Tom All that – it's . . . wrong.

Gary Stuff that's in my head. I don't fight it. I let it out. Thass your problem. What's in your head, Tom? Who do you want? The honey or the homo?

Tom I dunno yet. I want to find out. I gotta try different stuff.

Gary You wanna get online.

Tom You reckon?

Gary Yeah. You start searchin', chatting, message boards, stuff. You can try everything.

Tom Yeah?

Gary You wanna do a search now? 'Gay sex'? 'Battyman'?

Tom No.

Gary What you want?

Tom I don't know. Maybe I'll do Amy.

Gary You reckon?

Tom I could do if I wanted to, yeah.

Five

Tom *and* **Amy**. **Tom** *carries hair dye.* **Amy** *has a bandage round her wrist.*

Tom See? It's baby blonde.

Amy Right.

Tom I wanna go baby blonde.

Amy Right.

Tom And I want you to do it to me.

Amy I'm supposed to be doing my affirmations.

Tom What's that?

Amy I'm supposed to write out a hundred times 'I'm surrounded by love'.

Tom Why?

Amy Cos I cut myself again last night.

Tom Why?

Amy I dunno. I was bored. Or something. Or stress. I dunno.

Tom You gotta know.

Amy   I don't. Mum took me down the healer and she told me I had to do the affirmations.

Tom   You can do them later. Do my hair.

Amy   They don't work anyway.

Tom   No?

Amy   I did them before and they never worked.

Tom   What works?

Amy   I dunno. Melissa says I need a shag.

Tom   Maybe you do.

Amy   You reckon?

Tom   Yeah. I reckon.

Amy   There's no one fancies me.

Tom   That's not true.

Amy   Says who?

Tom   Says me.

Amy   Yeah?

Tom   You gonna do my hair?

Amy   If you want.

Tom   We need a bowl of water.

Amy   Alright.

Tom   And a towel.

Amy   Yeah yeah.

Tom   Thanks.

Amy *exits.* **Tom** *removes his shirt. Folds it up. Arranges himself on the floor. Pause. Enter* **Melissa**.

Melissa   Alright?

Tom   Alright.

Melissa   You seen my iPod?

Tom   No.

Melissa   She takes my iPod. Drives me mental. We're always having words. There'll be a ruck soon.

Tom   Right.

Melissa   You shagging?

Tom   Not yet.

Melissa   Do us all a favour and give her one, will you?

Tom   Do my best.

Melissa   Where the fuck's it gone?

Exit **Melissa**. **Tom** *arranges himself again on the floor to look as alluring and yet as natural as possible for* **Amy**. *Enter* **Amy** *with bowl of water and towel.*

Amy   I got it.

Tom   I took my top off.

Amy   Right.

Tom   Cos I don't want to get bleach on it.

Amy   Right.

Tom   That alright? Me getting naked?

Amy   Whatever. You got the instructions?

Tom   Yeah.

He gives **Amy** *the instructions.*

Tom   I've been thinking about what you said.

Amy (*reading instructions*)   Yeah?

Tom   About sorting myself out and that. In my head. You know – about whether I wanted . . . you.

Amy   You seen a therapist?

Tom   No. I just been thinking.

Amy   Right.

Tom   About who I wanna kiss and that.

Amy   Right. You got any allergies?

Tom   Why?

Amy   Cos it says here – (*the instructions*) You got any allergies?

Tom   Dust and peanuts.

Amy   Dust and peanuts should be alright. You wanna get started?

Tom   If you like. What if you got bleach on your top?

Amy   It's a crap top.

Tom   Yeah, but you'd ruin it. Bleach down the front.

Amy   Mum'll recycle it.

Tom   Maybe you better take your top off too.

Amy   I don't think so.

Tom   Go on. I took my top off. Time you took your top off too.

Amy   No.

Tom   Come on. Take it off. Take it off.

Tom *reaches out to* **Amy** *– she pushes him away.*

Amy   I'm not taking my top off, alright?

Tom   Alright. Do you reckon I should go down the gym?

Amy   I don't know.

Tom   Maybe I should go down the gym. My body's stupid.

Amy   No.

Tom   I've got a stupid body.

Amy   No. You've got a fit body. I like your body.

Tom   Yeah?

Amy   It's a nice body.

Tom   Do you wanna touch it?

Amy   I dunno.

Tom   Come on. Touch it if you like.

Amy   Alright.

Amy *reaches out to touch* **Tom***. Enter* **Melissa** *followed by* **Chantal***,* **Kerry** *and* **Alicia***.* **Alicia** *carries the baby.*

Melissa   Your mates are here. They're shagging.

Exit **Melissa***.*

Chantal/Kerry/Alicia   Alright?

Tom   Alright.

Amy   We're not – we weren't gonna –

Chantal   Thass a buff bod.

Tom   Yeah?

Chantal   For a kid, you're fit. He's fit, isn't he?

Kerry   He's alright. I mean I wouldn't –

Amy   We weren't gonna –

Kerry   But yeah, he's alright.

Amy   I was gonna dye his hair.

Chantal   Go on then.

Tom   Forget it.

Chantal   No. Go on.

Tom   Another time. I don't want people watching.

Chantal   It's safe. Go on. We heard you cut yourself again. You alright?

Amy   Oh yeah. I'm fine. Come on – let's wash your hair.

*Amy pours water over **Tom**'s head.*

Tom   Owww! Hurts! Awwww! Burning, aagh!

Amy   Shit.

Tom   What you – ? You put cold in that? You never put any cold in that.

Amy   I forgot.

Tom   You forgot. Shit. I'm gonna be scarred. Ugh.

Amy   I'll get cold.

*She runs out with the jug. **Tom** paces around scratching at his scalp, groaning. **Alicia** get out cigarettes.*

Kerry   Lish – don't.

Alicia   What?

Kerry   Not around the kid.

Alicia   Don't be stupid.

Kerry   It stunts 'em.

Alicia   Thass when you're pregnant.

Kerry   Not when you're mother.

*She takes the packet of cigarettes from **Alicia**.*

Alicia   Fuck's sake. I get stressed out without 'em.

Kerry   Yeah – well.

Alicia   See that, Spazz? Took my fags.

Kerry   Don't call it that.

Alicia   Whatever.

Enter **Amy** *with jug of cold water.*

Amy   Here.

Tom *kneels in front of bowl.* **Amy** *pours cold water over his head.*

Tom   Aggghhhh.

He lies back.

Amy   You better now.

Tom   Is there red? Like burns?

Amy   A bit.

Tom   Thought so.

Chantal   Are you gonna shag? Cos we can leave it you're gonna shag.

Tom   No. We're not gonna shag.

Chantal   You sure?

Tom   Yeah. I'm sure. We're not gonna shag. We're never gonna . . . no.

Six

Tom, Tarot Reader. *Nine cards spread out in a fan – three lines of three.*

Tom   And that one. What's that one?

Tarot Reader   That's the Tower.

Tom   What does that mean?

Tarot Reader   The Tower means . . . this is a time in your life when . . . the foundation on which – you see here these are your emotions – the foundation on which your emotions are based is unstable. It may collapse at any time.

Tom   Yes. That's how I feel. Nothing feels . . . fixed. I don't know who I am. I want to know. What does the Tower mean?

Tarot Reader   The Tower means change. You are facing a moment of great change. A moment of great decision. Yes?

Tom   Yes.

Tarot Reader   So. The Tower makes sense to you? You are facing a moment of great choice?

Tom   Yes.

Tarot Reader   All the time, we've got choices.

Tom   But how do we choose? They tell you choose – but how do you choose?

Tarot Reader   The cards. That's the way. My life. I was confused. I was lost. I got as low as anyone can go. The future was nothing but darkness and fear. But then – a gift. A stranger taught me how to read these signs and now I turn to the cards. Do you see?

Tom   I think so. Can we look at my future?

Tarot Reader   Of course.

Tom   Then let's do it.

Tarot Reader   Now this is – the cards are very strong here. The future is so –

Tom   Am I going to kill myself?

Tarot Reader   I don't see that. No.

Tom   Sometimes I wonder . . . pills and that. y'know. Maybe that's my future. When the pain gets really bad I . . .

Tarot Reader   No, no. You're a beautiful boy, you . . .

Tom   I mean, don't think I could, I'm too scared but if that's my future . . .

Tarot Reader   No. You will live a long life.

Tom   Right.

Tarot Reader   Are you pleased about that?

Tom   Yeah. Course. 'Spose.

Tarot Reader   A great, long happy life.

Tom   How? How? You say that to everybody –

Tarot Reader   I only tell the truth. If you can't believe me –

Tom   I just can't . . .

Tarot Reader   – the cards will tell us. They've always helped me. Here. Two of the major . . . we call these the Major Arcana, you see? Here – the pictures. The High Priestess – here. Drawing back the veil. Drawing back the veil to let you into her world.

Tom   It's a woman?

Tarot Reader   She's a feminine energy.

Tom   It's a woman letting me into her – I've got to know – that's a woman –

Tarot Reader   It's more complicated than that. We prefer the masculine and feminine energies.

Tom   But she's a woman?

Tarot Reader   Or a man with a feminine energy.

Tom   Oh.

Tarot Reader   Men can have feminine energy. You could have feminine energy –

Tom   No.

Tarot Reader   But your energy could –

Tom   What are you calling me? Are you calling me a girl? I'm not a girl.

He gets up and moves away.

Tarot Reader What are you doing?

Tom I'm going if you call me a girl.

Tarot Reader Alright. Go. If you have to – go.

Tom I will.

Tarot Reader Give me your money and go – but you'll never know – Here . . . the Lovers. The cards are so strong for the Lovers.

Tom The Lovers?

Tarot Reader Yes. You are about to enter the gate, pass the threshold and embrace the Lovers. A lover for you. Yes? You've got a question?

Tom I've really got to know. Sometimes I have these feelings for . . . Is it . . . ? I have a . . . lover?

Tarot Reader You do.

Tom Is it a . . . The lover is it . . . a man or a woman?

Tarot Reader Ah. I see. I can't tell you that.

Tom You have to tell me that. Tell me. Otherwise what's the . . . Please – please –

Tarot Reader I can't tell you that, but if you look at the cards. Look at the cards. Really listen to the cards. You are about to pass through the gateway and meet your lover. Man or a woman? What do the cards say? Look at them. Listen.

Tom I can't . . . Nothing.

Tarot Reader Make yourself comfortable. Be patient. Listen.

Tom No. I really can't . . .

Tarot Reader   We have time. You will choose a course of action. With the cards you will choose a course of action. Just watch and wait and listen.

Tom   Nothing. Nothing. No future. Nothing.

Tarot Reader   Ssssshh. Listen. Listen. Listen to the cards.

Tom *looks at the cards. Long pause.*

Tarot Reader   Yes?

Tom   Yes.

Tarot Reader   You know what to do?

Tom   I know what to do.

Seven

Tom, **Amy**. **Amy** *carries the baby.*

Tom   You got the baby.

Amy   She made me. Said I'd have detention for a week.

Tom   That's harsh.

Amy   Totally harsh. I told her – I'm not fit to be a mother, look at my arms. You can't be a mother when you've got cuts all over your arms.

Tom   And what did she say?

Amy   Said it would take me out of myself – think about another life.

Tom   Bit of plastic.

Amy   And now I have to write down all my thoughts and feelings in my baby diary.

Tom   What you written?

Amy   Nothing. Don't feel anything. It doesn't do anything. Just sits there. It's heavy.

Tom   Let me feel.

Amy   Go on then.

Amy *gives* **Tom** *the baby.*

Tom   Yeah. Really heavy.

He drops the baby.

Whoops.

Amy   You did that on purpose.

Tom   Maybe.

Amy   You're trouble.

Tom   That's right. Do you reckon it's damaged?

Amy   Shut up.

Tom *picks up the baby.*

Tom   No – it's fine.

Amy   Don't tell Kerry – she'll go mental.

Tom (*to baby*)   You're alright, aren't you? Aren't you? Yes.

Tom *throws the baby up in the air – lets it fall on the floor.*

Amy   You're mad.

Tom   I'm rubbish at catching. Catch it!

Tom *throws the baby to* **Amy**. *She catches it.*

Amy   I'll be bollocked if it's damaged.

Tom   Throw it to me. Come on.

Amy *throws the baby. He lets it fall to the floor again.*

Tom   Why can't I catch it?

Amy   You're not trying. Give it here.

She goes to pick up the baby. **Tom** *stops her.*

Tom   No – leave it.

Amy   Why?

Tom   Cos I'm here. You can hold the baby later.

Amy   What am I gonna write in my baby diary?

Tom   Make it up.

He takes his shirt off.

Amy   What are you doing?

Tom   I went down the gym. See?

Amy   How many times you been?

Tom   Three.

Amy   I don't think three's gonna make a difference.

Tom   Course it is. Have a feel.

Amy   Yeah?

Tom *flexes a bicep.*

Tom   Feel that.

Amy   Alright.

Amy *feels his bicep.*

Tom   See?

Amy   What?

Tom   It's stronger. Harder.

Amy   You reckon?

Tom   Oh yeah – that's much harder.

Amy   I dunno.

She picks up the baby.

Tom   Do you wanna have sex?

Amy   Maybe.

Tom   I think maybe we should have sex.

Amy   I've never had sex before.

Tom   Neither have I. I've seen it online.

Amy   Yeah?

Tom   Round Gary's.

Amy   Gay Gary's?

Tom   He's not gay.

Amy   Right. Are you gay?

Tom   Come here.

Amy *goes to* **Tom**. *He takes the baby out of her arms and lays it on the floor. They kiss.*

Tom   Did you like that?

Amy   Yeah. Is it me?

Tom   What?

Amy   In your dreams? Is it me you're kissing in your dream?

Tom   No.

Amy   Are you sure? If you can't see the face . . . ?

Tom   Yeah, well. But I can feel it.

Amy   And it's not me?

Tom   It's not you. Does that bother you?

Amy   No.

Tom   Good.

They kiss again.

Melissa (*off*)   Amy.

Amy   What?

Melissa (*off*)   You got my camcorder?

Amy No.

Melissa (*off*) You sure? I can't find it anywhere.

Amy I'm sure.

Melissa (*off*) If you've taken it again . . .

Amy I haven't taken it again.

Melissa (*off*) I'm coming to look.

Amy No.

Exit **Amy**. **Tom** *waits. Enter* **De Clerk**.

Tom How did you get in here, sir?

De Clerk Through the floor.

Tom What? You just . . . ?

De Clerk Come through the floor.

Tom Shit.

De Clerk Just something I can do. Don't tell the Head. We're not supposed to have special powers.

Tom Alright. Are you here cos I'm still a bit gay – is that it?

De Clerk Let's not talk about that.

Tom I sort of decided I wasn't gonna be gay any more – now you sort of – well, it's a bit gay, isn't it, coming through the floor like that?

De Clerk Are you going to have sex with her?

Tom Yeah, I reckon. What – don't you think I should?

De Clerk We can't tell you yes or no. That's not what we do.

Tom Why not?

De Clerk Because you have to make your own choices.

Tom But why? Everything's so confusing. There's so many choices. I don't feel like a person. I just feel like all these bits floating around. And none of them match up. Like a jigsaw that's never going to be finished. It's doing my head in.

De Clerk And what would you prefer?

Tom Someone to tell me what to be.

De Clerk No one's going to do that.

Tom I wish they would.

De Clerk When I was growing up: everyone told you who to be. They told you what to do. What was right and what was wrong. What your future would be.

Tom I'd like that.

De Clerk No. It made me very unhappy.

Tom I'm unhappy – too many choices. You were unhappy – no choices. Everyone's unhappy. Life's shit, isn't it, sir?

De Clerk That is I would say a distinct possibility.

Tom Are you still unhappy, sir?

De Clerk If I stop. If I stop working and rushing – the inspection, the continual assessment – trying to pay the mortgage every month, trying to please the Head, trying to get home before nine every night – then, yes, I'm unhappy. But only when I stop.

Tom You've got a boyfriend?

De Clerk I can't talk about that.

Tom You're gay, sir. I don't mean that in a bad way. I just mean – like you know who you are. And you're gay. I'm going to have sex with her.

De Clerk If that's what you want.

Tom So you better get back through the floor. I'm not having you watching us.

De Clerk I don't want to watch. Use protection.

Tom I know.

De Clerk If you're having sex, use protection.

Tom That's telling me what to do.

De Clerk It's advice.

Tom It's telling me what to do. You should tell me more of that.

De Clerk I can't. Promise me you'll use protection.

Tom I might do.

De Clerk Promise.

Tom Do all gay people come through floors?

De Clerk Now you're being silly.

Enter **Amy**.

Amy She's gone now.

Tom Good. (*To* **De Clerk**.) You going?

De Clerk Take care.

Exit **De Clerk**.

Tom Is everyone out?

Amy Yeah. They're all out. Got the place to ourselves.

Tom That's good.

Amy Are you scared?

Tom A bit. Are you?

Amy Scared and excited.

Tom We'll take it slow.

Amy   Yeah. Let's take it really slow. You got anything?

Tom   Like what?

Amy   Like condoms and that?

Tom   No.

Amy   Oh.

Tom   Does that bother you?

Amy   No. Does that bother you?

Tom   No.

Amy   Do you love me?

Tom   I don't know. Maybe later. Is that alright?

Amy   Yeah. That's alright.

Tom   After – we can do my hair. I still want blond hair.

Amy   Alright.

Tom   Turn the light out.

Amy   I want to see you.

Tom   No.

Tom *turns the light off. The* **Baby** *comes forward and speaks to the audience.*

Baby   And so it happened. My mummy and my daddy made me that night. Neither of them enjoyed it very much. But they did it. And that's what they wanted. And that night I started to grow in my mummy's tummy. And by the time she did her GCSEs I was almost ready to come out of her tummy.

I think that night as they lay together in the dark she thought they might spend all their time together from that day on. But that didn't happen. In fact, once that night was over, they were sort of shy and embarrassed whenever they saw each other until – by the time I was born – they weren't speaking to each other at all. And Mummy says for a few moments – she's sure there were a few moments that night when he did really, really love her. And I believe her.

They did talk to each other once more after they left school – but there's one more bit of the story to show you before we get to that.

Eight

Tom *and* **Martin**. **Tom** *has a hat pulled down, completely covering his hair.*

Tom   You've got a nice place.

Martin (*off*)   Thank you.

Tom   Yeah, really nice. Trendy.

Martin (*off*)   Thank you.

Tom   What do you do?

Martin (*off*)   My job?

Tom   Yeah. Your job.

Martin (*off*)   I'm a systems analyst.

Tom   Right. Right. Is that alright?

Martin (*off*)   I enjoy it.

Tom   And the pay's good?

Martin (*off*)   The pay is ridiculously good.

Tom   Well – that's good.

Martin (*off*)   And you?

Tom   What?

Martin (*off*)   Do you have a job?

Tom   Yes.

Martin (*off*)   What do you do?

Tom   Well, actually, I'm looking.

Martin (*off*)   I see.

Enter **Martin**, *with two bottles of beer. He gives one of the bottles of beer to* **Tom**.

Martin   Cheers.

Tom   Right. Cheers.

Martin   If you want to take off –

Tom   I'm alright.

Martin   Maybe – your hat . . . ?

Tom   No.

Martin   Alright.

Tom   It's just I had a disaster.

Martin   Yes?

Tom   With my hair.

Martin   I see.

Tom   Yeah, this mate tried to dye my hair but it went wrong.

Martin   Right.

Tom   Yeah, tried to dye my hair, but I had a bit of a reaction and it's gone really weird, like ginger bits and green bits and that. Last month. I'm waiting for it to grow out. I look weird so that's why I'm wearing –

Martin   It suits you.

Tom   Yeah?

Martin   The hat. It's a good look.

Tom   Thank you.

Martin   You're a good-looking guy.

Tom   Right.

Martin   Was it your boyfriend?

Tom   What?

Martin   With the hair dye?

Tom   No.

Martin   Have you got a boyfriend?

Tom   No. Have you?

Martin   Yes. Is that alright?

Tom   I suppose. How old are you?

Martin   Twenty-one.

Tom   Right.

Martin   How old are you?

Tom   Eighteen.

Martin   You said nineteen in the chatroom.

Tom   Did I?

Martin   Yes.

Tom   Well, I'm eighteen.

Martin   But actually you look younger.

Tom   Really?

Martin   You actually look about sixteen.

Tom   Everyone says I look younger. That's what they said when I was at school.

Martin   Right. Do you want to come through to the bedroom?

Tom   In a minute. Are you happy?

Martin   What?

Tom   You know, in your life and that? Does it make you happy?

Martin   I suppose so.

Tom   With your boyfriend and your job and that?

Martin   I never really think about it.

Tom   You seem happy.

Martin   Then I suppose I am.

Tom   That's good.

Martin   And you?

Tom   What?

Martin   Are you happy?

Tom   I reckon. Yes, I am.

Martin   Well, that's good. Look, we really should get into the bedroom –

Tom   Right.

Martin   My boyfriend's coming back at five and I don't want to –

Tom   Right.

Martin   Sorry to hurry you, but –

Tom   That's alright.

Martin   You can keep your hat on.

Tom   Thanks.

Martin   You're cute.

Tom   Thanks. I've never done this before.

Martin   Chatrooms?

Tom   This. All of it.

Martin   Sex?

Tom   No. I've done sex. Only . . .

Martin   Not with someone so old?

Tom   Not with . . .

Martin   Twenty-two too old for you?

Tom   No. Not with . . . a bloke. I mean, I did it with girls, a girl, but . . .

Martin   Did you like it?

Tom   It was alright.

Martin   If you like that kind of thing.

Tom   Yeah. I'm shaking. Sorry. I feel nervous. Is it gonna hurt?

Martin   Not if we do it right.

Tom   How will we know?

Martin   I don't know. You just have to . . . er . . . suck it and see.

Tom (*laughs*)   You dirty bastard.

Martin   Yeah.

Tom   I shouldn't have come.

Martin   Alright then – another time. How are you getting back?

Tom   No, no.

He kisses **Martin**.

Martin   Mixed messages.

Tom   You're right. I'm sixteen.

Martin   I know.

Tom   I'm legal.

Martin   What do you want?

Tom   This.

He kisses **Martin.**

Tom   Come on then. Where's the bedroom? Or do you want your boyfriend to find out?

Martin   The bedroom's through there.

Tom   Your boyfriend, he's not . . . ?

Martin   Yes?

Tom   He's not . . . is your boyfriend a teacher?

Martin (*laughs*)   God, no. He's a mortgage broker. Why?

Tom   Nothing.

Martin   Ready?

Tom   Ready. Just – don't touch my hat, alright?

Martin   Alright.

Nine

Amy, Tom.

Amy   Your hair's alright.

Tom   Yeah. Took a few months. But in the end it went back to normal.

Amy   You should still do an earring.

Tom   You reckon?

Amy   Yeah. I always reckoned an earring would really suit you.

Tom   Maybe one day.

Amy   Yeah. One day. What you up to?

Tom   Not much. I'm going to college next year.

Amy   That's good.

Tom   Fashion.

Amy   Nice.

Tom   And I'm doing coat-check.

Amy   In a club?

Tom   Sort of pub-club.

Amy   Gay club?

Tom   Just Fridays and Saturdays. You should come along.
It's a laugh.

Amy   You got a boyfriend?

Tom   I dunno.

Amy   You got to know.

Tom   There's a bloke . . . We . . . meet up. A couple of
times a week. But he's living with someone.

Amy   His boyfriend.

Tom   Yeah. He's got a boyfriend. He keeps on saying
they're gonna split but they haven't. Still – we have a laugh.
He's got money.

Amy   Right.

Tom   You seeing anyone?

Amy   Yeah.

Tom   Who?

Amy   Nosy. I mean, I can't go out much but, you know, if
I get a babysitter –

Tom   Right.

Amy   I'm gonna do college in a couple of years.

Tom   That's good.

Amy   Just gotta wait till she's a bit older.

Tom   Of course. If you need me to babysit –

Amy   No.

Tom   I don't mind.

Amy   I've got mates do that for me. Kerry loves it.

Tom   Yeah, but if you ever need me to –

Amy   I don't need you to.

Tom   I want to.

Amy   I don't want you to, alright?

Tom   Alright. I still . . . think about you.

Amy   Right.

Tom   Like . . . fancy you and that.

Amy   You told your boyfriend?

Tom   Sometimes, when he kisses me, I think about you. He kisses me but I close my eyes and it's your face I see.

Amy   You can't have it both ways.

Tom   That's what I want.

Amy   Well – you can't have it.

Enter **Gary**, *pushing a pram.*

Gary   Alright, babe?

Amy   Yeah. Alright.

Gary *kisses* **Amy**.

Amy   She been alright?

Gary   Yeah. Fast asleep the whole time.

Amy   She'll be awake all night now.

Gary   You want me to wake her?

Amy   No. Leave her alone.

Gary   Alright, Tom?

Tom   She told me she was going out with someone.

Gary   You guess who?

Tom   No. You gonna bring the kid up to be a stoner too?

Gary   No. I give up the weed, didn't I? Can't be blazing around the kid, can I? Once you got a kid to look after – that's the time to grow up, I reckon.

Tom   Yeah – suppose that's right.

Amy   Tom's gone gay now.

Gary   Thass cool.

Tom   Can I have a look at her?

Amy   We gotta go in a minute. Mum's booked us up the naturopath.

Tom   I just want to have a quick look.

Amy   Go on then.

Tom   She's beautiful.

Amy   Yeah. She's alright.

Tom   Can I pick her up?

Amy   No.

Tom   I'll be careful.

Amy   I don't want you to.

Tom   Alright.

Amy   Not now she's settled.

Tom   Alright.

Amy   Best to leave her alone.

Tom   Alright.

Amy   I want to keep her out of the sun.

Tom   Of course.

Gary   We've got to get the bus.

Amy   Yeah.

Tom   Will I see you again?

Amy   Maybe.

Tom   I wanna see you again. I'm the dad.

Amy   Gary looks after her – don't you?

Gary   Yeah.

Tom   Yeah – but still.

Enter **Martin**.

Martin   Sorry, I tried to get away only –

Martin *goes to kiss* **Tom**. *He steps away.*

Tom   Don't.

Amy   You his boyfriend?

Martin   I wouldn't . . . sort of . . .

Tom   Yeah. Only sort of.

Amy   Better than nothing though, isn't it?

Martin   That's right.

Amy   See ya.

Exit **Amy** *and* **Gary** *with pram.*

Tom   Did you tell him?

Martin   What?

Tom   You know. About me. You were supposed to tell him about me.

Martin   He's away this weekend. What do you want to do?

Tom   Do you love me?

Martin   You know I don't like to use that word.

Tom   Because?

Martin   Because.

Tom   Tell me.

Martin   What does it mean? It doesn't mean anything. 'Love'? It doesn't mean . . .

Tom   You've got to say it.

Martin   No.

Tom   There's no point to this. There's no point to anything. What's the point?

Martin   Money. Sex. Fun. That's the point.

Tom   No. I want –

Martin   What?

Tom   Say you love me.

Martin   No.

Tom   Say you love me.

Martin   No.

Tom   Say you love me. Please. Please. Please – say you love me.

Martin   Okay. I love you – okay?

Beat.

Tom   . . . No.

Martin   Fuck's sake. Why can't you . . . moneysexfun?

Tom   Because I want more. I want everything. I want . . .

Martin   Yes?

Tom   I want everything and I want . . . I want . . . I want to find out everything.

Martin (*laughs*)   You're a baby. Treat you like a baby.

Tom   No. Not any more. No.

pool (no water)

A Frantic Assembly, Drum Theatre Plymouth and Lyric Hammersmith Production, *pool (no water)* was first performed at the Drum Theatre Plymouth on 22 September 2006. The cast was as follows:

Keir Charles
Cait Davis
Leah Muller
Mark Rice-Oxley

Direction and choreography   Scott Graham and Steven Hoggett
Design   Miriam Buether
Lighting design   Natasha Chivers
Music   Imogen Heap

The original production had four speakers – A, B, C, D. Other productions don't have to follow this.

A pool, she had a pool.

Of all of us the most – at least in the eyes of this so-called world – the most successful of us.

So – a pool.

Did she mean to impress? Was it for show?

No. I can't think. No. Because she's . . .

She's good. She's nice. She has integrity. Her roots.

And she has a pool now – it's fantastic fantastic fantastic fantastic.

But she hasn't forgotten us. Visits to rehab. Visits to hospices. Visits to Aids wards. She's made them.

And she comes to our exhibitions. Cramped little exhibitions in lofts in the bohemian quarter. Our photos, our *objets trouvés*, she comes, she sees, she sometimes buys. And she'll help our fund-raising drives.

She's tireless in her help for our fund-raising drives.

We adore her. We adore her. We all absolutely adore her.

Years ago when she was in – when she was in the Group. Life and soul. And she'd always be ripping her clothes off, just ripping them off, and we'd all rip them off too – we'd follow her – and then we'd all make performance pieces or arthouse shorts or we'd just go skinny-dipping for the sheer naked fun of it.

But nowadays she's . . . absent.

Exactly. She's . . . absent. It's that quality in her work that sells. The pieces that first began when we lost Ray to the whole Aids thing. And she used Ray's blood and bandages and catheter and condoms. Pieces that sold to every major collector in the world.

Aha.

Absent. And yet somehow – recognised by the world.

Aha.

And now she has: the pool. The poooooooooool.

First seen in attachments. A Christmas attachment. Open the attachment for a PDF of my new pool.

I open with caution. I have a fear of viruses.

Her pool. 'You're welcome at any time. Come over, share the pool. Any of you – singularly or together – just come over and enjoy the pool.'

And there's the PDF. There's the pool. Clean and blue and lit by beautiful lights. And there's the pool boy – who could have been a porn star. Or maybe is a porn star. Or will be a porn star. And there's her personal trainer taking her through her lengths. And he's a porn star too. And maybe the pool boy fucks the trainer. Or the trainer fucks her. Or she fucks the pool boy.

No no no no – she's always been a very moral person. She's always had a strict code of morals. Even in the hovel days. She never did the hah-hah-heroin for more than a day. And she always kept her door strictly shut at night.

And so we email each other back and forth: yes, let's go and see the pool, let's go and share the pool, why not? Why not? Let's share it with her.

And we email her back. We're coming, we're coming, we're all coming. We're all getting on a plane and coming over to share the pool with you.

And she Es back: Fantastic. Fantastic. Fantastic.

Time drifts, of course. We're all busy – there's exhibitions in the bohemian quarter, there's a project to provide murals for heroin babies, there's fund-raising there's –

There's Sally in the hospice. Sally in that fucking hospice. It's got into her bones now, it's eaten through her body and now that little evil cunting C is eating into her bones – it's got a taste of marrow – and she lies there and she says:

I want to die I want to die all I want is to die why can't they just let I won't take the medication when all I want is to die?

And we say to her

Think of the pool. Think of the pool. That's something to keep going for. We'll get you out of here and fly you out to the pool. Fantastic healing healthy happy times ahead at the pool.

And she says

Yes.

But that's just to humour us. Nobody believes that.

And Sally turns green and Sally turns grey and there's a drip drip drip stuck everywhere and nurses and nuns and we organise a rota because life must go on with its exhibitions and its fund-raising and we take it in turns until we all rush there one night and some of us make it and some of us don't and that's Sally done for.

And you're just stripped naked because suddenly all the art was worth nothing, it is nothing, it means nothing. Sally has gone and Art did nothing and Art could do nothing and Death is big and we are small and really we're nothing, we're nothing.

And *she's* there at the crematorium. And she says: Thank you for looking after Sally. Thank you for that. You were all amazing for looking after. I'm so guilty. I should have been here sooner. And we're: no no no no no.

But I felt did you feel, listen I felt, this is wrong I know this is wrong but I felt, maybe it's only – did anyone else feel – and it is only a feeling, but a feeling is a feeling and I think that should be honoured, you know? If you know what I'm saying? Okay, okay, I'm going to say it, I'm going to tell you, I'm going to tell you what I what I felt, standing in the crematorium and suddenly she's there with her Manager or whoever the, she's there and I want to scream at her: Cunt.

God.

Yes, just open my lungs and scream at her: 'Cunt. Cunt –
this is your doing. You did this. You see this casket? You see
this casket, see this cheap horrible wooden casket with our
friend Sally in it? You did that. That was you.'

God.

'It was you who killed Sally.'

God.

'Because none of us was meant to be wealthy, none of us
was meant to be recognised, none of us was meant to fly.
We're the Group. And there's balance. And you took away
the balance. One of us goes up, then one of us goes down.
It's a natural law. Don't you understand the most basic
natural law? Well of course you do – understood it and
ignored it – on purpose – and killed Sally. Chose to kill
Sally. Cunt. Cunt. Cunt.' And if I could I would have torn
her hair from her head and torn the clothes from her body
and spat into her cunt right then and right there. That was
what I . . . Did anyone else . . . ?

No no no no one else. I see. I see. I see.

You see, what bad people. We are all bad people. It needn't
be that way of course. No. It needn't. If only we'd use our
Art for some good. But instead we harbour . . .

And I think maybe have always harboured, you know right
since the hovel, harboured . . .

Now we reflect . . .

Isn't that strange? All the time she was amongst us as a
friend, all that time and yet really we harboured the most
awful . . . well I suppose *hatred*

Murderous hatred

Would be the only word.

Well that's awful. That is truly terrible.

Yes it is – and we must let that go. We must. Both with our work with the heroin babies, but also in our attitude to her. We must embrace her. We must love her. We must move forward and let go of the past and let go of the badness and move forward with our love for her.

'You're all wiped out,' she says. 'You're all exhausted,' she says. 'Physically and spiritually and emotion. Please come out to the pool. Please. Please. Come on. It's the least I can do.'

And so we all say: yes.

Oh let's leave hatred let's leave death let's leave that behind. The poooooool.

And we go.

It takes so many hours to fly to this strange new world and there are palm trees and heat haze in the dusk of the airport.

And she's there:

Welcome welcome welcome.

And in the huge hallway of the house there's the pool boy and the personal trainer and the cook:

Hello. Hey. Hi. Welcome. Good to. Yeah. How ya? Come on make yourselves anything I can? Fantastic. So you're? Heard so much. That's good.

And yes – we feel a little guilty when we think of all the suffering back in the city – the beatings and the orphan and the pain – and for a moment we want to rush back there and make some art. But we take a moment, take a moment to let that pass – because really are we responsible for every baby whose mother is a junkie? That would be vanity.

And we look at her and we see . . . Yes, really you're just a person. A person like us. And – why did we feel those terrible things all these years? Oh, it feels good to have let them go. And we notice how graceful her movements are

and how beautiful her laugh sounds and we actually rather
adore the way she's not so present – so pushing herself at
you – so *there* as other people are.

And we each of us hold her and say: 'It's good to be here.
It's great to see you.' And we actually mean it. And we are
lighter than we have been for years.

You know she's a marvellous person. One of us, out in the
world and doing well. It's time to celebrate that.

And that night there's a meal – swordfish and watercress
and cool cool wine and we get reminiscent and we get cosy
and we get tearful. About the – God, do you remember
when we are all together when it all seemed to mean so
much when everything was so full of meaning yes it was all
drenched in meaning and we all cared we all cared so so
passionately? Do you remember do you remember do you
remember do you remember do you remember the days?
Ah yes happy happy happy happy happy happy happy days.

I remember . . . very bright colours. In the crib. In the
school. In that first studio we shared. I remember everything
having so much colour that I felt: 'God, how can I ever find
a medium that has so much colour?'

Time for bed.

And each of us is in a bed.

But suddenly she's there, suddenly her head is round the
door:

'I know we said sleep but I thought skinny-dipping let's
come on skinny-dipping in the pool before bed.'

God she hasn't lost it despite everything despite all this
grandeur she's still . . . naughty naughty naughty.

Magic words from long ago: sk-iii-nn-eeee-dippp-pinnnggg.
And we're back out into the night and we're giggling and
we're drunk and there's no light in the grounds there's no
light on the pool everything's been switched off. And we say:

clothes off. Because isn't that the naughtiest, most alive, most wonderful . . . ? Clothes off.

And we take off our clothes.

And each of us knows that our body is not what it was those ten years before – that there's sag and fat and lines even and even even the littlest hints of grey. Oh yes the sad sad rot to the grave has already begun.

But that doesn't matter in the darkness. In the darkness we're as we were ten years ago when we strip poker and performance pieces and all that naked fun.

And it's just so beautiful. Slightest breeze around your cracks, hanging a little in the wind.

And some of us cry and some of us laugh but we're all moved by the sheer naked beauty of it.

I'll always remember that moment, always. Just something . . . all of us standing there naked in the dark. Sometimes now when the painkillers aren't working I try to visualise that moment and then things don't seem so awful.

Come on she squeals come on the pool!

And then she's running and whooping through the darkness and she launches herself and you can just see her up in the sky, up against the sky, the arc of her body through the night sky up and up and up and up.

She seems so high. She's flying. She's an angel. A drunken laughing goddess angel.

And then she arcs down and we're clapping and we're cheering.

And then

Some of us thought we heard the splash. You do. When you think there's going to be a splash then you hear a splash. You do the work. But we didn't hear the splash. There was no splash. There was

The crack

The cracking of her body.

The harsh crack of her body against the concrete.

Then there was silence.

Then there was her groan and her squeal and her screams of pain.

Aaaaaaggghoooowooooowoooowwwwwww.

We edge forward in the darkness our naked figures moving forward in the dark until we're at the edge at the pool. And then we see, see as our eyes adjust

Pool. No water.

Just hints of water in a pool now drained.

And there in the middle of the concrete her body twisted and crunched and crushed and her noise now animal no more of god or angel. Ooooaaaaaawwwww.

We don't speak. We don't look at each other. We're too together now to need to look or speak to each other at all.

And we climb down and we climb down into the pool.

And we stand around her.

She was still conscious then. Still screaming and crying and jerking.

And we wanted to feel what she was feeling — she is one of us, we are artists — no, we're people — we wanted to feel what she was feeling — share the pain.

But it didn't happen.

We stood. We stood and we watched the jerking and we heard the screams. And we stood and we watched. All of us.

We couldn't do anything. Couldn't touch her. But we could have felt something. A life without empathy is . . .

She didn't jerk for long. She . . . went. Did she die? I
suppose for a moment it crossed my mind and I was – no
she didn't die and I think somehow we knew she didn't die.
She 'passed from consciousness'.

And the great absent thing is lying at our feet and we're
thinking:

This is right. This feels – there is right in that.

I'm sorry you had to suffer, I'm sorry there's this pain – but
there is justice in this. Something is shaping our ends.

For Sally, for Ray, for us, this had to be.

You see you flew – yes – you reached out your wings and
you flew above us. And that's okay. You tried and
congratulations. For trying. But you thought that could last?
Flying above the ground, looking down on our lives in the
city below? You really thought that could last? Of course
that couldn't last. And now you've crashed right down. And
that hurts doesn't it? I understand. That hurts.

This feels good. This feels wonderful. Look at you. Hah.
Hah. Just look at you. I am great.

There is strength in me. Oh the strength in me I never knew
I had.

You bitch you bitch you bitch you bitch you bitch you bitch
you bitch.

And we

Maybe you will die. Maybe death will come for you. And if
it's come for you, it hasn't come for me. That's me saved for
another day.

And we

You shit you shit you evil evil evil evil shit to think these
things of another person what kind of evil lies inside you?

And we

You've patronised my. You've patronised my exhibitions in the bohemian quarter. At last at last I can patronise you. I can care. What better way to patronise you back than care for this mangled crippled body?

And her face. You would have thought – locked into a grimace of pain, intense emotion. But no – her face on top of that crunched-up body her face was as absent as it had ever been. And if I could have drilled into her skull – or ripped it off – just to know what thoughts and feelings went through her head, then I would. I swear to God, I would.

There's a little stream of piss comes out of her now – green from all the wine. And it's the – funny to think of it now – it's the piss that focuses our minds.

And we organise and we call and we open doors and we're – you go in the ambulance I'll follow in a –

Oh please take care of my friend. Please. The most awful accident. Please.

As in that room she's wired up and dripped up and hooked up and we come and go and bring each other coffee and cigarettes and we pace the corridors and we ask the doctors and the nurses for news news news any news? We would never dare tell each other just how – and this is the word – exciting this is.

Did you feel that – ? I wish there was something else but there was –

The excitement that all of us deny. Because excitement is not – no, not an appropriate response.

'It's touch and go with your friend,' the doctor tells us. 'It's distinctly touch and go.'

Come on you cunt feel oh feel oh – but we look – we look like we're supposed to look, we do the – the little tilt of the head, the little sigh, the tear comes down the cheek – just like we know it should.

Her body – her body is broken in our head. A picture but not – it's not a feeling you know? And you would have thought above all else an artist would –

And in the room one of us or all of us – anyway somebody says to her:

'You can't hear but I have felt the most awful things towards you. And that won't continue. It can't continue. You are down and I am going to care for you. Please let me in and I will love you. Don't be absent. Be here. Please.'

And back in her house we lay our heads down and we see them parading through our room – Sally with her breast eaten away, Ray with a lung no bigger than a matchbox and now this – and we want to join the parade and march down to hell or heaven or purgatory but we don't because we have a diazepam and a smoke, a wine and a diazepam – and that's okay.

The next day the personal trainer sobs. The cook howls. The pool boy threatens an overdose. The boy who drained the pool without notice the boy who – We console them. We are all benificence. We discover – oh wonderful – what good people we are.

And of course as soon as we humanly can we go to the hospital.

We can't remember now. It doesn't matter. Oh of course it matters to curators it matters to historians. But to us it doesn't matter at all. But one of us first thought of taking a camera.

We don't even know who first packed the digi-digi-digi-digi-cam for our visit. Maybe we all did.

But there we are – hospital with the camera in our hand.

And we're here. We're here. We're here in the room with the camera and the sunlight coming through the blinds.

Hello. Hello. It's us.

Please wake and stop us. Don't let us do that. You don't
have to burble on. Just open your eyes. That's all. Do you
know how much we used to – you were just so much a part
of us and now . . .

And we hold the camera down by our sides.

Come on. Just look. And see. And feel. And care. It's a
natural human thing. But we . . .

And you see now – look – what it's done to her. Now the
blood's been cleaned away. The body bruised and swollen
into shape no other human's yet achieved. Her limbs in
plastic. Her neck in plastic. Her mask. The drips and the
tubes. And the machines that inhalate and beeeep. A
moving . . . a timeless picture of the . . .

Our friend yes but also . . .

The line of the machine . . .

The purple of the bruise . . .

It appeals. It tempts. There is beauty here. We know, we've
spent our life hunting it out and there is beauty here.

And we stand and we look and at last we're moved by the
intense beauty of that image.

(Throw camera – disgusting thing – through window and
eight floors to the street below.)

If you'd been in that room with us then maybe, maybe
you'd have felt the same. Because today we are all artists.

And the light was good and the potential for composition
was all there – and to be honest it was easy easy easy easy to
come up with those images that so later seemed striking.

(Stamp on that lens and shit on that viewfinder and tear the
memory out by the soul.)

And the temptation to arrange – just to move the bed . . . so
. . . so the composition was . . . get her head in the light, so.
The temptation was great and we were weak. So we wheel

her into light and actually move the limbs and head –
checking of course not to disrupt the tubes and drips and . . .
science and art can work together happily.

It took a few moments to snap. An image a record a frame.

Later, we sat in the smoking room and said to ourselves:

That wasn't a good thing to do. That was a terrible thing to
do. Why not select delete and wipe away what you've . . . ?
Why not?

And we did. No – honest with you – we nearly did. But we
never did.

And that night on the laptop we survey our work and we –
ah – we are not disgusted with ourselves as we expect we
should. We are already thinking interviews – exhibition –
catalogue – sale.

The next two months. The daily round.

The morning to the hospital wait for your chance collect
your images while you can.

Oh how well we get to know that hospital! And for a while
I actually dated the nurse – Miguel – we had blood tests to
check for infections and confided the results but I wasn't
ready to commit so that ended. And I think Miguel might
actually have suspected – there were some questions – about
the daily photos. Not that there was anything wrong . . .

Still we were furtive for that whole time. Maybe just for the
thrill . . .

Then evenings back to survey what we've done.

Start to arrange, start to order, start to catalogue. Start to –
print with a quality of drenched colour, tone and definition
and . . .

Her home is our home, our studio. And in the morning the
sun rises on us and at nights the sprinklers bless the lawn
and we are fed and attended to by her staff.

And my body – during that time my body starts to rise and
tauten as the trainer comes at six and we run through the
suburbs to that gym and in the afternoon I swim fifty lengths
in the pool.

I wish I'd had a nutritionist before. I feel fabulous.

And in time – the right dealer, the right agent, the right
publicist – this will be an important series of images.

We've become fascinated by the – look you can see –
fascinated by the way the markings and the bruisings and
the cuts progress from day to day.

Just look. Just look. Just look and see. Isn't that rather
interesting? Isn't that fascinating?

The way the bruises and the swellings grow and ripen over
her. The myriad colours that a bruise can take. One day an
eye revealed and then another concealed beneath the
swollen. Yes.

And we feel together. We feel as one. There is a job of work
to do and we are doing it.

Oh we are alive – would you look at that, the old corpse is
back from the brink – and I'm shaking a stump and I'm
walking the earth and I'm breathing the air.

Hurrah! Hurrah! Hurrah!

Don't sing it too loud but

Hurrah! Hurrah! Hurrah!

Join me if you will

Hurrah! Hurrah! Hurrah!

We're the Group! We're the Group! We're the Group!

But happiness is . . . Happiness is so fast. Eight weeks and
then . . .

We arrive as usual. And Miguel – we weren't dating by now that had finished some ooo – Miguel comes forward and he is smiling at us. Beaming.

And we know, we know. We can say the words for him.

'Your friend is conscious.'

Oh.

Two months and Sleeping Beauty is . . .

Oh.

And I felt light because . . . because that had been . . . what was that – ? Taking those images? Snatching that . . . ? No no no no. That wasn't a thing that we were supposed to do. That was a . . . oh relief relief. This is . . . saved. I am so happy that art has gone away and now we can be people.

That is wonderful.

Let her be present. Please. Let her be . . .

I did a line before I went into her room. I never told anybody that before. I knew I had just enough for a line and in the nappy-changing facility I . . . I don't understand myself.

'Hello. Look it's us. We're all here.'

She's not awake – not awake like you and me – she's slipping in and out – but sometimes her eyes open and she'll look at us and she sees us. She's in the room with us. once she even gives us her smile. I swear to God.

And we're happy. For her. But also for us. A quiet happy but still . . .

And we talk that hospital talk that burble that you talk to the semi-conscious and to babies. We burble a nice sound because she deserves the sweetest baby talk.

'We're going to go skinny-dipping. Any day now. That's what we're gonna do. We're gonna get you out of here. And we're all gonna strip and it's going to be back . . .

. . . You will be one of us just as it was all the decade past everything stripped away and us just a bunch of cunts of dicks and titties and bumcracks us the bathing beautiful oh think of that my darling think of. We are so lucky to have known and we'll know it again. We will. We will. We will.'

I kiss her. She doesn't do anything. But that's okay. Everything is . . .

And we say to each other: It's over. She's mending. Happy days are coming.

And we hold hands and we smile and we hug and we sing. The Group stand around her bed and we sing and she opens her eyes and she looks at us and . . .

I think for a moment . . . no.

Yes I thought . . . I don't know whether anyone else thought . . .

Maybe all of us thought . . .

She knows. She knows what we have been doing. She sees the camera in our pocket and she understands. How much wiser than us she is.

But that couldn't be.

So we hold the water to her lips and we stroke her fingers and we breathe:

We love you.

And she says:

Thank you for being my friends through all of these years.

And – no – she didn't know that thoughts of hate had ever gone through our heads and we are – well – blessed – and – um – absolved by those words. And that feels very good.

And for hours we are there with her as she sleeps and wakes and I think this was the . . . calmest I have ever been in my life.

So why – back at her house did we start to – ? I let the gym slip those weeks. My belly sags.

I drive-thru and the chicken wings and ice cream until my stomach burns.

One night with lots of wine and spliff and cokeycokeycoke an actual row. Subject – nothing. But screaming and slamming and tears and silence.

And actually you know it's at moments like this that I find that my depepependcy issues really emerge? Because I want to – oh Counsellor – I want to be part of the Group that's what I want so much but if they won't maybe I've excluded mmmm ah shit there's no fucking needles in this fucking room what's a hospital room without a needle you know?

And the – I'll give you a hundred to sleep with me. Leave the pool for a moment. Leave the pool alone just for one goddam minute and give me one good fuck won't you? What is wrong with my money?

And Ray and Tommy and Sally are rattling around in my room. Call it a drug-abuse-related issue if you like. But I call it grief when the bones of dead friends are banging against your head and drowning out the sounds of life, while we . . . Eat. Sleep. Shit. Wank. Begin again. Eat. Sleep. Shit. Wank. Begin again.

Oh yes. That's right. One of us decided to show her the images. Well – I can't remember which . . .

I don't think it was me but . . .

Maybe I could have . . .

Anyway one of us – we were – what? – all in the room and there was something about her smile then, the way she looked at us as we cared for her.

I felt like she was accusing me and I . . .

It's so hard to know what she's thinking. Always been like that. But normally you feel like she's . . . judging.

And I just wanted . . .

Somebody thought: I have to tell her. To make myself feel better.

Maybe to hurt her.

And she was looking down at her body – still purple and twisted – and she says:

'No mirror anywhere. I must look like shit. I guess they don't want me to see what . . . '

And there was a voice:

'Oh you can see what you look like.'

'Yes?'

'But maybe you shouldn't. Maybe it's best.'

'No. I'd like to see.'

She didn't stop us you see, there was every chance.

'You've got a mirror?'

'No but . . . '

The laptop out. That first week in the hospital. She's barely human. Scroll. Week two, three, on through the months. She begins to heal.

And she's watching. But I couldn't see . . .

Still nothing in her eyes.

And then she asks:

'Where do these come from?'

And so we: We took them.

And I thought she'd understand the evil inside us. But I really don't think she did because anyway she says:

'Thank you.'

Like she means it.

She didn't want us to put the laptop away. But we did. The battery was running flat.

And then she says:

'Can you take me to the toilet?'

They'd removed her catheter by then and so I supported her to the toilet and I felt okay because I was holding her and she really needed me.

And you know there were visits when she didn't mention the images. I don't know – three? four? – several visits when they didn't come up.

In my mind several weeks when they were unspoken. And I suppose actually it wasn't wrong, it was – what's the word? – kind to record that for her.

Well yes, if we'd done it for her. Yes. And if we hadn't arranged the body. Planned the exhibition. If we could forget.

And then one day she says:

'Bring the camera.'

'Oh . . . no.'

'Yes. Bring the camera. I want to carry on. I'm still healing. I'm getting stronger all the time. And I'd like to carry on recording that.'

What could we do but bring the camera?

She laughed that day. She was so happy. She turned her head into the light to show the bruise. She pulled up the gown to show the wounds, the stitches, the bone almost sticking through the blue flesh.

She is driven by an energy we haven't seen for years.

'You stand over there. Here – get the drip in the frame beside the cuts on the hand.'

And we carry out her commands. So many images and then:

'Let me see let me see let me see myself.'

It's an order. Delivered like a child but still . . .

And so we scroll through and she studies intently and oh . . .

That's the kind of moment when any sane person needs a K hole you know? Just to get you out of that room.

And she likes them.

And all that energy.

Every day she drives us on. And every day is recording her.

The old routine was naughty. She was sleeping. We were snatching bits of her. And now . . .

It is our job to make her happy. And she loves this. And she grows stronger every day. While we . . . we actually started to feel rather sickly you know?

I have headaches. I have migraines. This morning I slipped while shaving and see the see the cut. No it's alright but yes yes actually it does actually sting. But you mustn't worry about me. Doctor doctor I think the pool boy may have passed on something fungal. I'm yeasty and I want to cry about it.

We want her to sleep. We don't want her to tire herself. She should be sleeping all the time but now . . . we are the exhausted ones. The visits to the hospital. The fluorescent light. That bad coffee. It is very tiring.

And now she wants hard copies. So we provide hard copies.

And she lays them out around the room, arranges, rearranges, studies. And – yes – sometimes she does ask our opinions but really it is her eye, her eye shaping them into a form.

She is so good at what she does. She has shown at such fantastic galleries. You actually learn from her working her way through those images. Which is a privilege.

But we still have to take her to the toilet. Remember. At the end of the day . . . we still have to take her to the toilet.

It had never crossed our mind that she might have other visitors so when we saw . . .

Tall. Rich. Tanned. Bit of a cunt.

'Who was he?'

'He owns the gallery that I work with out here. We've been talking about the work I want to show when I get out of here.'

What work?

'Oh . . . just ideas.'

But I knew. It was lost then. It was her body. She had dived into the pool. It was her act. And we thought we took the images but she was the work. And she has everything and we have – oh – nothing.

I can't do this any fucking longer you know? Give me a break. Let me succeed.

She would claim the images and we would be back in the bohemian quarter doing – oh – very good work with the underprivileged. But be honest – I've done my dues – I want to be privileged.

And now it feels like punishment to take those daily images of her. You can hear what will be said about her. You know who will buy these.

I must do something else with my life. But what?

So have a party in her room. Spliff away. Let's feel as though we're all together in this and making these pictures. Let's really do everything we can to feel that.

And now the time comes. It's winter. She's coming home.

Excitement. Something we can organise.

She's made a list of course. Clothes and make-up that we have to take to prepare her. In we go. She's sitting on the bed, expectant, ready now to go. Clothes on with some assistance make-up artfully applied.

And walking through the ward she looks so strong so well. Amongst the injured dying lines she looks so strong as if to insult each of them one by one. And it's us following behind who look the weaker. The weak ones stepping in her step.

But on the street – where the healthy ones parade around and flirt and deal and hustle and threaten – well there – even as she passes through the revolving door and into the rain – suddenly she seems the weaker. Suddenly you see the way her limbs are now not set quite right, the drag and hobble of her frame. You see the way no make-up known can quite conceal the swollen face. Just one step from hospital to street – but all the difference. And she's the stranger here. This is our world – despite the shabby little lives we've led – this is our world and she's not quite finding her feet.

And we are good again. We are good. As we help her into taxi, give directions, hold her as a bump or turn inflicts a little pain upon her. We're here for you, we're guiding you, we love you. We're taking you through the darkness. Trust us. Love us. Please.

She's tired at home. She takes in banners cakes the pool. A little smile. That little smile she's always given year on year and never given anything away. The smile that you can make of what you will. But the smile done she's dozing and we say:

Come on to bed to bed to rest that's what you need it's all so much you need to rest.

And we watch over her and we do care for her. We do
genuinely – it's very important that you should believe this
bit – we do genuinely care.

There's interrupted sleep. She's seeing it again and again
when her eyes are shut. Slipping off the clothes. The leap
into the air. The arc up and up into the stars. Swoop down.
And then the instant of concrete. The instant of knowledge
of all the pain that must come and then – crack. And she's
awake.

But we're there. There's always one of us there. And she
smiles and says

Thank you thank you thank you thank you for being here.

And we say:

Silly you silly no we want to be here.

And it's true. We do. We really do.

And she has visitors. Her manager. Her publicist. The
gallery owner.

And we welcome them and we show them up to her room.

And we smile at them and offer them drinks and we can't
make out the words of the conversation that is going on
above our heads.

But really we know. We know that this story. Her story. The
pictures. This is what they are dealing in. Selling.
Packaging. Promoting. Launching. They are getting ready
for the launch day.

And we are housemaids really and any day now we'll be
deported home.

And look honestly years ago who would have thought . . . ?
She was the least of us honestly.

Then one day she

Let's get out the images. Let's put them out around the room.

Here we go. Here we go. She's preparing. So we . . .

No no you're not ready you're not ready for that not while you're getting better no not now later we can go through them.

Promise?

Of course of course we promise you.

And that was meant. We meant it then. Nothing hidden then.

I wouldn't say the virus was willed. It wasn't quite as clear as that. No one of us actually sat down and said

Come you virus come enter in my inbox spread your stain through modem into memory and mainframe come.

That would be ridiculous. But I do think one of us in our heart of wretched hearts knew that the attachment was a dupe, knew that opening 'read me' would wreck the laptop file by file, taking out the images – zap zappy zappy zap.

We protested

Shit shit shit

But we hadn't backed up so . . . something going on more than just a freak.

Didn't tell her. Kept on

Rest now and when you're then the images yes yes yes.

And we hadn't lost them all. The bulk had but there were some still in the camera memory a few hard copies left. Enough to piece together even if – even if – even if –

Well even if chunks of – great big chunks of actually – whole chapters of – some key bits of the – even if 'read me' had actually fucked up the story of her healing so now she healed in leaps and starts – a nonsense narrative.

But there was a kind of – still enough to satisfy her need no doubt.

And the day was coming. The day was coming now. The day when we had promised her that she could see the images laid out from the first stolen shots of her swollen mangled totally unconscious frame right through to those final few days – the final rush of wellness in the hospital.

Tomorrow we tell her tomorrow. Tomorrow you will come down and it will all be presented in the living room – the gallery of you.

Thank you

She says and off she drifts sleeping with the calmest smile you've ever seen.

And we sit in silence. Waiting for . . .

Oh God.

Waiting for . . .

I blame the personal trainer. He wouldn't be the first – is there a personal trainer in this world who doesn't deal as well as train? But it was the personal trainer who dealt us the stuff that night. He was selling but yes okay and we were buying.

I thought I was clean I really thought I was so clean. But I'm not. I never am. Never will be. I'm a user and I always will be. Until the day I die. Isn't that great? Isn't it fucking great? Because I know who I am. This is me. I'm a userjunkiecuntcrackwhorefeelmyKholecuntedtwat that's me and it feels . . . fucking great.

I am alive I am alive. Sober is dead. The faces of the fucking sober dead and I am so fucking from my cunt to my arse to my tits to my mouth I am fucking alive.

Kiss me kiss me somebody stick a tongue in me or up me or I don't fucking care come on humans let's human each other or sniff cracks I don't care let's be human isn't that

great with the this is are you up? I'm up and up and up and
up and cunted and cunted and c-c-c-c-cunted. Woah!
There's no fucking coming down now.

Turn the music up turn the music up turn the music up turn
the music up I want my stomach to bleeeeeeeeeed when you
turn the music up.

And then one of us produced the camera, produced the
memory. Choose our first image and

Delete

Oh yes oh yes oh yes oh yes oh yes.

And then a great wave of fun

Select Delete Select Delete Select Delete Select Delete
Select Delete Select Delete Select Delete Select Delete
Select Delete Select Delete Select Delete Select Delete
Select Delete Select Delete Select Delete Select Delete
Select Delete Select Delete Select Delete Select Delete
Select Delete Select Delete Select Delete Select Delete
Select Delete Select Delete Select Delete Select Delete
Select Delete Select Delete Select Delete Select Delete
Select Delete Select Delete Select Delete Select Delete
Select Delete Select Delete Select Delete Select Delete
Select Delete Select Delete Select Delete Select Delete
Select Delete Select Delete Select Delete Select Delete

Until not a single memory of the 'miracle of healing' left.

A little pause then as we drunk in what we'd done. A little
chance to celebrate how strong we are now. God – the
triumph pumping through our torsos.

But look . . . there's the hard copies. Yes the hard copies.
The last remaining bit.

Let's stop now. It's done now. We know we are strong. We
know it.

I'm coming down. Look at me. I'm coming down actually.
Fuck I need water.

Oh no we're up now. Please let's . . . please don't let this end.

This is the only thing we will ever do on this planet and we know that. Our lives are nothing. Our work is nothing. No be honest with ourselves fucksake our work is nothing.

And our work is nothing and we are no people. We have ruined our lives. We took a wrong turning into art and it has taken us nowhere and it's too late now to discover our talent.

And look at our bodies look at them my tits are jjjjjust moving every day towards the grave.

And I wish I had Aids or cancer – Sally lucky Ray lucky – Aids or cancer so I didn't have to suffer the slow drip-drip-drip-indignity of the everyday drag of life.

So – don't turn back now. Don't do that.

Pedro – come back over here and bring as much fucking gear as you've got we'll buy the lot.

Alright my friends alright. This is it. Music please from every speaker. Stick a bit of porn on the plasma and it's . . . chemical roulette . . . whatever you pull out the hat you inject or inhale or you stuff up your arse.

Here we go here here we go here h – h-h-h-h-h-h – here weeee g-g – g-gooooo!

And the lighter – the first flame on the corner of the first image of her healing. We whoop and laugh and are delighted at the flames flaring up and blanking it away.

Taking it in turns now

Let me burn I'm next I'm the next to burn

The bonfire

And we dance we dance about in total free free freedom as the images away in guttering and fumes and blaze.

It's going it's going it's going soon be nothing left.

What's going on?

She's there. Just a T-shirt and she's in the doorway.

What are you doing?

And we want to say:

You know you know you know what we're doing. Surely you know you knew we had to?

But we don't. We stand and watch her. Silence. She's moving in. She takes the centre. And she takes it in. And sees.

And she understands then – she knows.

Everything she thought was friendship was hate. Everything that was care was envy. Concern was destroy. And we hold her in her hands and we have snapped her neck and we have broken her legs and we have trodden on her skull.

And finally. Oh finally she is absent no longer. She is totally . . . there. And her eyes take us in. And it's as if we can hear her say – her mouth is closed, but still I, we, I we, heard:

'You are small people. You have always been small people. Ever since the day. There are small people and there are big people. And I am a big person and you are not. Yes? Yes? Yes?

'Oh I've held this in all these years but no more.

'I have talent. I have vision. I am blessed.

'None of you can ever touch me.

'You thought I didn't see all your jealousy and hatred all these years? Of course I saw it.

'And Sally and Ray died because they were too weak to live, to live and and make art.

'I am the only one of you strong enough ever to really live and nothing you can do will ever destroy me. Because I will always be the stronger.

'So write to me please from time to time and let me know about your small lives.'

And you know when she said it – such a relief that she wasn't absent any more after so many years.

And really – oh really – it was.

And so really I suppose it was one of the happiest nights of my life.

No actually it was the happiest night of my life. To have somebody tell you the truth like that . . . try to get somebody to do it to you if you can . . . try it tonight . . . it's really fantastic.

And now. Years have gone. And look at these arms – no track marks – nothing. Clean. And these four here – new teeth. Beauties.

And I actually met someone who I rather like and I have two children – one is two, the other is four – and they like me so that makes it feel rather better. Because when we're all playing around the paddling pool things seem rather okay. And the children have their own little mobile phones – for safety – and they like to take pictures of Mummy lying in the pool. And that's lovely.

And I like to think there's a rehab or an Aids ward or a somewhere where we'll be together once again. Somewhere where we'll meet and be the gang. But – hey I'm a romantic. I'm a foolish old romantic as the years go on.

So. Light the candles. Bake the cake. Sing the song. The gang's all here. We're here together. And the dream is dreamy and oh life is long.